T0341332

ROUTLEDGE LIBRARY EDITIONS:
FOOD SUPPLY AND POLICY

Volume 8

FOOD SUPPLIES IN THE AFTERMATH OF WORLD WAR II

FOOD SUPPLIES IN THE AFTERMATH OF WORLD WAR II

EDITH HIRSCH

Routledge
Taylor & Francis Group

LONDON AND NEW YORK

First published in 1993 by Garland

This edition first published in 2020
by Routledge
2 Park Square, Milton Park, Abingdon, Oxon OX14 4RN

and by Routledge
52 Vanderbilt Avenue, New York, NY 10017

Routledge is an imprint of the Taylor & Francis Group, an informa business

British Library Cataloguing in Publication Data
A catalogue record for this book is available from the British Library

ISBN: 978-0-367-26640-0 (Set)
ISBN: 978-0-429-29433-4 (Set) (ebk)
ISBN: 978-0-367-27580-8 (Volume 8) (hbk)
ISBN: 978-0-429-29677-2 (Volume 8) (ebk)

Publisher's Note
The publisher has gone to great lengths to ensure the quality of this reprint but
points out that some imperfections in the original copies may be apparent.

Disclaimer
The publisher has made every effort to trace copyright holders and would welcome
correspondence from those they have been unable to trace.

FOREIGN ECONOMIC POLICY OF THE UNITED STATES

Food Supplies in the Aftermath of World War II

EDITH HIRSCH

GARLAND PUBLISHING, INC.
NEW YORK & LONDON • 1993

Library of Congress Cataloging-in-Publication Data

Hirsch, Edith, 1899–
    Food supplies in the aftermath of World War II / Edith
Hirsch.
        p.   cm. — (Foreign economic policy of the United
States)
    Includes index.
    ISBN 0–8153–1197–4 (alk. paper)
    1. Food supply—Government policy. 2. Agriculture and
state. 3. Food supply—Government policy—United States.
4. Agriculture and state—United States.   I. Title. II. Series.
HD9000.6.H5   1993
338.1'973'09045—dc20   92–46744
                                                            CIP

Printed on acid-free, 250-year-life paper
Manufactured in the United States of America

To my granddaughter, Claudia Hirsch.
Her broad perspective, rapid understanding
and inexhaustible energy transformed a research
project of long ago into this present-day book.

Contents

List of Figures

List of Maps

List of Tables

List of Abbreviations

AAA	Agricultural Adjustment Administration (U.S.)
CCC	Commodity Credit Corporation (U.S.)
CFB	Combined Food Board
FAO	Food & Agriculture
IEFC	International Emergency Food Council
OFAR	Office of Foreign Agriculture Relations (U.S.)
OPA	Office of Price Administration (U.S.)
SCAP	Supreme Commander, Allied Powers (Japan)
UNRRA	United Nations Relief & Rehabilitation Administration
USDA	United States Department of Agriculture

Foreword

This study was written in 1946, i.e., shortly after the end of World War II. It was commissioned by a large American corporation which was a client of my consulting partnership; I was its agricultural economist. The raw materials for the corporation's product line were largely grain and various other agricultural products. Our client corporation was understandably concerned about the continued availability and price of its raw materials.

In the past, wars often produced starvation that outlasted the hostilities, and in fact there were some real food shortages in parts of Europe and the Far East during the latter half of 1945 and early in 1946. However, by the time this study was written (July and August of 1946), a careful look at the available data showed that there would be no serious food shortages in the then-current crop year nor in the coming ones.

That, however, was not the perception of the key officials of agencies such as the United Nations Food and Agriculture Organization (FAO), the U.S. Department of Agriculture (USDA) or of some private American agribusiness experts. They felt that the 1945/46 food shortages would last for many years and that therefore world-wide agricultural planning should be implemented as soon as possible.

If implemented, those policies would have amounted to a set of universal food controls. Food surpluses and deficits would have been equalized world-wide, and international controls would have been put in place to guarantee farmers' incomes and to administer the distribution of fertilizer, feed and farm machinery.

My research showed that those views were utterly wrong, and that the food shortages of the immediate post-war period were caused by unprecedented conditions highly unlikely to recur. It convinced me that free markets and the price mechanism would quickly restore normal conditions and that the main agricultural problem would then again be oversupply, which had already plagued the world's economies before World War II. Government action should not be to administer food production and distribution, I felt, but rather to help food-deficit nations to help themselves: to use American loans and other crèdits to finance purchases from the United States not of food, but instead of seed, draft animals, farm machinery, fertilizers and equipment for chemical fertilizer factories.

My views were not shared by agricultural administrators abroad, by the FAO or by the USDA, but they were soon confirmed by events, such as the collapse of Britain's "Groundnut Scheme,"[1] and others. Thus when I made my first postwar visit to Europe in 1948, I found that rationing had been reduced to vestiges and that food availability was generally very good (except in Paris [sic], which was impacted by the first of many farmer protests against the French government's agricultural policies). Similarly, in Denmark bread was rationed, not because it was in short supply but to discourage farmers from feeding it to their cattle: the price of bread was subsidized to the extent that it was cheaper than regular cattle feed. Shortly after my visit, bread rationing ended — but the bread price was raised!

------

1. A British government program during the years 1947-1953, operated in collaboration with British industrial groups. Its purpose was to meet an anticipated shortage of edible oils and to provide jobs for Africans who had fought for the British in World War II. Jungles in East Africa were cleared and converted into peanut (Brit.: groundnut) plantations, and plants were built to convert the peanuts into edible oil. Clearing the jungle and constructing the oil plants ran into severe logistic difficulties which caused cost and time overruns. By the time peanut oil production began, oversupplies had caused the world price of edible oils to collapse. The program was abandoned amid recriminations that went on for many years.

Even today, the European Economic Community's "butter mountain" and "wine lake" continue to provide confirmation. The world's economies still face many problems, true, but food shortages do not rank high among them. When and where they do appear, such as currently in the Horn of Africa, they are exceptional and usually the result of political upheavals or other human-made circumstances. They are no longer confirmations of Malthus' dismal prophecies, which have proved irrelevant, at least for the 20th century. We have grounds to believe that they will remain that way.

Edith Hirsch
Washington, D.C.
November, 1992

HERBERT BAYARD SWOPE
745 FIFTH AVENUE
NEW YORK 22, N.Y.

9 September 1946.

Dear Dr. Hirsch:-

Your report was printed under a big splash on the first page of The London Daily Express of September 3d. I am trying to get a copy for you.

Lord Beaverbrook cabled that he was enthusiastic about the work, and that the Conservative party wanted to use the report in full. I have given permission to do so and have asked if they want to use the name of the author. Do you wish me to supply this detail?

Lord Beaverbrook's paper termed the report "brilliant and exhaustive."

My warm regard.

Herbert Bayard Swope

Dr. Julius Hirsch,
52 Wall Street,
New York City.

Highlights of the Study

Three principal conclusions arise out of the accompanying study of demand for and supply of food throughout the world this year and in the future:

1. The hunger crisis of the spring of 1946 was caused by unprecedented conditions which will not recur, and the crisis is just about over already.

2. The world's food supply for the coming year will cover all real shortages, and beyond 1947 the primary problem of all phases of agriculture is very likely to be, as before the war, what to do with our plentiful farm production — not how to increase it.

3. In spite of these facts an attempt is being made to build up the consumption controls on grain, flour and their products, which were introduced and maintained for an emergency now almost past, into a *permanent world-embracing planned food economy.*

Under the leadership of the Food and Agricultural Organization of the United Nations (FAO), supported by strong adherents of planned economy in the United States and by socialist and labor governments in Continental Europe and Great Britain, a plan for world-wide control of food has already been projected. This plan, published July 6th, contains definite recommendations not only for what is Biblically called "the lean year" (1946/47) but also directly for 1947-8 and indirectly for two more years.

The purpose of the supporters of this plan is revealed to be (see Chapter 2) the automatic equalization of world surpluses and deficits, but without giving any decisive consideration to the ability of deficit countries to pay. Another aim is an international guaranty of income for farmers in all countries and an international control of the distribution of fertilizer, feed and farm machinery. The AAA thus would be expanded to embrace the globe and to control the principal industries serving agriculture. The plan is scheduled to be presented by the chairman of the FAO at its next meeting, set for September 2 in Copenhagen.

This whole idea derives dangerous strength from the sudden and totally unexpected nature of the hunger crisis, which tends to cause many people to fear that it might recur at any time. Accustomed for many years to think of the farm problem solely in terms of surpluses, they were painfully jarred loose from that comforting assurance. It will take time, and the real facts to restore their equanimity.

The crisis was caused (see Chapter 1) by quite extraordinary circumstances which no one could foresee. A destructive drought occurred in five vast areas of food production. The effects were seriously aggravated by actual warfare and by the devastations of the war. It is most improbable that such a disastrous combination of events will ever occur again.

The sudden threat was met and overcome almost entirely by the large grain surpluses of North America, and by redistribution of available food organized under the leadership of the United States in a few weeks' time. The possibility of any repetition of the emergency in the crop year 1946/47 can be discarded completely.

Predictions by the FAO and by the British Labor Government as recently as July 4 must be revised in the light of unexpectedly favorable crop reports from all parts of the world. This fact has already received partial recognition officially. In its July 28 report to the President's Famine Emergency Committee, the Department of Agriculture's Office of Foreign Agricultural Relations (OFAR) said that Europe bids fair to come within 90 percent of its prewar average for food production this year. It puts world wheat prospects almost up to the prewar average, or 700 million bushels more than last year.

Thus, while an improvement in conditions is registered, there is certainly no sign as yet of the proper interpretation of this fact.

While in May the FAO and our own OFAR estimated that for the world as a whole in 1946/47 there would be an excess of needs over supplies amounting to at least ten million tons of wheat equivalent, the accompanying study demonstrates that *no deficit at all will exist,* even if no dependence is placed on oats and corn to supplement wheat. If there should be a minor gap in wheat, the large prospective surplus of coarse grains in North America and Argentina this year will be sufficient to close it by applying food standards developed in actual practice.

All in all, therefore, most of the government restrictions on use of grains and their products which are still in effect here and in other surplus countries, *are progressively losing their raison d'être.* Once the wheat crop is in — and most of it is already — and the record corn crop is no longer subject to weather accidents, the removal of these restrictions will become a matter solely of expediency. It is possible that the political atmosphere just before election will provide the necessary incentive.

The *key to the coming year's grain supply lies in the number of animal guests at our national table.* If the livestock numbers on farms are large they eat grain which otherwise might be used directly by humans, and the food value of the amount of meat and fat they provide is several times smaller than that of what they eat. Fortunately, the livestock population in this country is smaller than at any time since the war, and it is physically impossible to increase it until next spring's pig crop arrives. Therefore, barring a drought during the next three weeks, we have absolute assurance that this year's huge output of grains will not be eaten up by our animals during the months when it will be most needed for export to deficient countries.

It is true that if the supply of corn becomes large enough to drive down the price, it will become profitable to feed it to animals rather than to sell it, and farmers will be moved this fall to plan a large crop of pigs for the following spring. But those pigs will not become big eaters until almost nine months from now. In the meantime, the supply of grains is ample. (Chapter 3.)

The *needs of food-deficit* countries also are turning out *to be not as great as assumed in the official estimates* made in May. While the accompanying study reaches the same figure as the FAO, that is, eight million tons of wheat equivalent, for the import requirements of England, the Middle East and Latin America, it finds revisions necessary for Continental Europe. This study, based on a country-by-country survey, puts it at a maximum of eight to nine million. This takes into account the special needs of the non-Russian zones of Germany and Austria and also of Poland, where political problems are delaying adjustment and recovery. Surprising as it may seem, Russia may actually favor rather than oppose the export of grain from the Danubian countries.

Consequences of the grave crop failures in the Far East late in 1945 will continue to be felt for two or three months. The Hoover Committed allocated for those countries from May to September of this year a total of 4.8 million tons of wheat equivalent, but our study shows that the larger part of this allocation has not yet been delivered and that part of it will be supplied from 1946/47 crops. In China, unfortunately, transportation difficulties, complicated by civil war, are so great that the delivery of more than one million tons to the starving people in the interior is impossible this fall. Finally, crop reports from the Far East show considerable improvement, there is no sign of drought this year, and large quantities of previously hidden rice have made their appearance in Thailand and Indo-China.

These various factors together lead to the conclusion that an import total of 7.5 million tons will be the maximum which can realistically be estimated for the Far East for the crop year 1946/47. The total for the three regions is thus 24-24.5 million tons compared with the FAO's figure of 30.5 million, and that amount is exactly matched by our estimate of the exportable supply of wheat and rice from surplus counties. In addition, we can see an available supply of corn and oats equivalent to 5.6 million tons of wheat.

Other food problems dealt with in this study include that of meat and meat animals, in which Europe is seeking to rebuild depleted production; fats and oils, supply of which will continue tight; sugar, where supply likewise is recovering rather slowly; and fish, which will definitely be caught more plentifully and will substitute for other protein in Europe and Japan.

American national policy recommendations of this study include the following:

a. *Food Scare propaganda at home and abroad,* and attempts to perpetuate an international egalitarian economy of compulsion *should be fought.* Some practical proposals are given in Chapter 5.

b. Abroad we should seek primarily to *help the food deficit nations help themselves*. Instead of food let us rather send overseas the means of food production such as seed, draft animals, farm machinery, fertilizers and equipment for chemical fertilizer factories. Our big loans and other credits could be used in part for the improvement of antiquated agricultural techniques and for reclaiming acreage from heaths, swamps and the sea. They could also be used to supply the vastly scarce commodities like cotton goods, which the farmers would be glad to obtain in exchange for food crops.

c. If any government controls are continued, they should carry on Secretary of Agriculture Anderson's policy of encouraging production of non-animal food and holding down numbers and weight of livestock, which are a much less efficient form of food production. This would help obviate any fears that food scarcities might recur, and any losses sustained by the Federal government in holding up grain prices for that purpose would be small indeed compared to the size of our postwar budget.

The prospect of renewed surpluses in later years, mentioned at the beginning of this summary, rests on the enormously increasing use of fertilizer, which can have tremendous impact, and the improvement of seed, which in the case of corn is the cause of our huge crops of the last few years. When we add to this the great increase in and perfection of agricultural machinery, we observe three consequences vital to the nation:

First, the output per employed person in agriculture, which from 1939 to 1945 rose by 50 percent or 60 percent, will continue to increase.

Second, the numbers of people working on farms will continue to decline as in the last 15 years.

Third, output per acre will increase.

The greatest problem after 1947 will be to promote use of the best soil in order to add even further to efficiency of farming and consequently rising standards of living. Even more important will be the increasing use of farm staples for industrial purposes made possible by the discoveries of organic chemistry. Farm products may be destined one day to become America's most valuable source of industrial raw materials.

Food Supplies in the Aftermath of World War II

Chapter ONE

Why the Food Emergency
of 1945/46 Will Not Recur in 1946/47

Causes of the Emergency of February 1946

At the beginning of 1946 the world found itself faced with a food shortage far worse than anything experienced during the war. Failure to recognize this shortage before the beginning of the second half of the crop year increased its actual impact and naturally intensified its psychological effects.

By late summer of 1945 requests for exports of wheat from the United States were only 225 million bushels, while an export of more than 400 million bushels was badly needed. Only because of the very energetic action of the United States, and the very great carry-over, plus excellent harvests both here and in Canada, was it possible to save the world from starvation.

The severe shortage in the 1945/6 crop year arose from the coincidence of the following misfortunes:

1. *Actual warfare* took place in several countries at the time of the sowing and harvesting: Germany, Austria, Poland, the Danubian states and Czechoslovakia, thus had much smaller harvests. So had Thailand and Indo-China. In some areas the soil was not cultivated at all in 1945.

2. There were *severe droughts* in five regions: Australia; the Far East, including India; South Africa; the Mediterranean countries; and Southeastern Europe.

3. In Argentina and Australia *smaller grain crops* had been planted during the war. Because no shortages were expected, no efforts were made to increase the acreage.

4. There was an *acute shortage of fertilizers*, of labor and draft power.

5. *Heavy looting* of the available stocks occurred in many of the liberated and the occupied countries.

6. Since it was expected in fall of 1945 that the world supply would be approximately adequate, there was *premature relief from restrictions* on food and feed consumption in some countries. The bread rations were increased, and because it seemed desirable to build up the reduced livestock herds, grains which could have been used more advantageously directly for food were fed to animals. Great Britain, which during the war had increased the cultivation of wheat and potatoes, returned to the production of more feed.

7. There was no *world-wide planning*, in spite of the Combined Food Board, and in many cases not even nation-wide planning.

On the other hand, there was one great advantage: The carry-overs of wheat amounted to about 600 millions bushels for the United States and Canada, while it will be at best 200 million bushels the year.

Why No Repetition of the Emergency Is Likely in 1946/7

Fortunately we do not need to expect a repetition of these events. While there are still severe shortages in the meat, fat and sugar supply the world over, and while there will scarcely be anything like a general over-supply of grains in 1946/47, there should be enough food in the present crop year to allow for adequate diets in most countries and to avoid starvation in all of them. Even some rehabilitation of the depleted livestock in Europe might become possible.

The favorable developments which have brought about this outlook, are as follows:

1. *The crop weather has so far been excellent.*. Both in our own country and in Canada we can expect new bumper crops of wheat and small grains. Our own corn crop will be the largest ever if the weather is fair in August. The weather has been favorable in France, in the Balkans and in all Mediterranean countries, which suffered so heavily from drought last year. No droughts have developed thus far, except in the Ukraine, where replanting was partly possible, and in New Zealand. If the favorable crop reports from Russia hold true, exports from the Balkan countries to Western Europe possible.

2. Since commodity prices have risen considerably since last year, *Argentina* and *Australia* are planning *much larger crops* than last year. High grain prices all over the world act as an incentive.

3. *The soil has been fully cultivated* with few exceptions in all European countries this year. This also holds true for most of the Far East although timely imports of cotton goods could still perform miracles in producing rice.

4. *Fishing* has already been expanded. Fish will be a supplement to otherwise low-protein diets throughout the 1946/47 crop year, both in Europe and in Japan.

5. There is full awareness, or perhaps over-awareness, that food is still in scarce supply. In the various countries the available supply of indigenous and imported food will be apportioned over the whole year, so that deficiencies in the last months of the crop year will be avoided. Also, there is full cooperation among the countries. It can be expected that the real needs will be known in time, and appropriations made accordingly.

6. The available *grain will carry farther*, since the extraction rates have been higher from the very beginning of the crop year, while in the 1945/46 crop year they had to be raised in the second half. Wherever it is possible, wheat will be blended with grains in greater supply, such as oats, corn and also with potatoes, or with soybean cake. Our own very good oat crop will help to this end where needed.

Thus, except for the possibility of bad weather in August, which would affect our all-important corn crop, and for unexpected droughts in the Southern Hemisphere, the world will escape starvation without too great sacrifices on the part of this country, although, on the basis of gift exports and credits, world demand may yet outrun world supply in some commodities, though not necessarily in bread grains. There will be a lack of oil-seeds from the Far East. Oilseeds, the bulk of which came from the Far East in prewar times, were second in importance in world trade only to wheat.

Because of this deficit of oilseeds, which means less fats and fewer dairy products, some form of international cooperation in the distribution of available supplies of food, fats and oils will no doubt continue to be necessary for some time.

The General Answer to the World Food Problem in 1946/47

In May 1946, the FAO drafted the following:

World Food Balance Sheet for 1946/47[1]
(in million metric tons wheat or wheat equivalent)

Import Needs

Continental Europe including French North Africa	12.5	United States	6.8
Far East including India	10.0	Canada Argentina Australia	9.2-11.2
United Kingdom, Eire, Brazil, other Latin American and African countries	8.0	Others	2.0
	30.5		18-20
rounded to	31		

[1] Report of the Special Meeting on Urgent Food Problems, FAO, Washington, May 20-27, 1946.

The gap, as assumed by the FAO was 10 million tons.

The remedies for closing this gap which the FAO proposed were a series of drastic restrictions for all nations, continuing not only through 1946/47 but extending into 1948, and providing for

World Food Balance Sheet
FAO vs. Estimates
(in million metric tons—wheat or wheat equivalent)

Import Needs

	FAO—May 1946	Our Estimate
Continental Europe including French North Africa	12.5	8.5
Far East including India	10.0	7.5
United Kingdom —Eire—Brazil —Other Latin Ameri., African Countries	8.0	8.0
Total	30.5	24.0

Available for Export

	FAO—May 1946	Our Estimate
Wheat United States	6.8	8.0
Canada Argentina Australia	10.2	13.0
Others	2.0	2.0
Rice Surplus (outside Far East)	1.0	1.0
Oats & Corn (for food)		5.6
Total	20.0	29.6

the ultimate development of an internationally controlled agriculture thereafter.

An *alternative remedy*, seldom mentioned in contrast to the emphasis given to the numerous restrictions, is quoted by FAO as follows: "*If only 5% of the coarse grains for feed could be saved and exported, 7.5 million tons of food grains would be available.*"[1]

The forecast given above was made on the basis of crop estimates of April of this year and under considerably higher nutritive standards than applied by the Hoover committee or by the Allied occupation authorities. The findings of our report, based on statements by Herbert Hoover and on ample material compiled up to July 23, 1946, including that of the United States Department of Agriculture (USDA), arrive at the different figures on the preceeding page:

These figures show that the real import requirements in Continental Europe will not be 12.5 million metric tons of wheat as estimated by the FAO, but about 8 to 9; not 10 million in the Far East, but Near East and Africa of 8 million are added, the total is 24 to 24.5 million metric tons.

Exports of wheat and wheat flour of the four main exporters have been estimated at 20.5 to 22.8 million tons, and for the Danubian countries and others at 1 to 2 million tons. This does not include exports of rice from the United States, Brazil and Egypt, which amount to about 1.0 million tons; nor are exports of coarse grains included. It seems that almost any deficiency of grain for human consumption can be made up by coarse grains, since we are expecting the largest crop of feed grains ever harvested in the United States. This crop may even be sufficient to allow for an increase in the export of coarse grains for feed purposes.

Danish Government Expert Foresees Enough Food For All in 1946/47

The total prospects certainly justify the statement of the Danish Government expert, A.P. Jacobsen, which rather excited the majority of the members of the FAO at a meeting of May 21:

I am inclined to believe that the aggregate acreage cultivated in the whole world is not much lower than before the war . . . It can hardly be doubted that the coming harvest will be big enough to procure a fairly sufficient amount of food for all people. It depends entirely on how the harvest is used.

Corrected World Food Balance Sheet 1946/47 as of Mid-July 1946

(in million metric tons)

Import Needs		Available for Export				
Wheat		**Wheat**				
Continental Europe including French North Africa	8.5–9	United States	300–325m. bush.*	= 8.0–8.6 million metric tons		
		Canada	275–300 " "	=7.3–8.0	" " "
Far East including India	6.5	Argentina	100–120 " "	= 2.6–3.2	" " "
		Australia	100–110 " "	= 2.6–3.0	" " "
United Kingdom, Eire, Brazil, other Latin American and African Countries	8.0		775–855 " "	= 20.5–22.8	" " "
		Danubian Countries and Middle East	37.5–75 " "	= 1.5–2.0	" " "
	23.0–23.5			**22.0–24.8**	" " "
		Rice going to the Far East		1.0	" " "
		Total Wheat and Rice		**23.0 – 25.8**	" " "
Course Grains For India	**1.0**	**Course Grains** For Food	200 m. bush.	= **5.6**	" " "

---

*including 30 million bushels in the hands of the governments from the previous harvest.

Since Mr. Jacobsen made this statement, crop conditions have improved to such a degree that drastic regulations will not be necessary, at least in the surplus countries, to prevent starvation in the world.

Outlook for 1947/48

For the crop year 1947/48 the increased application of chemical fertilizers here and abroad, of mechanical power, of better seeds and progress in the reconstruction of European and Far Eastern agriculture make the recurrence of an emergency improbable. This could only happen in case of a serious drought in North America. Surpluses in some commodities are very likely.

The year 1948/49 might bring the problem of surpluses, though in that year some replenishment of the "ever-normal granary" will still be desirable. In the years that will follow, this problem will surely be with us. It should be met by a positive policy of improved nutritive standards, higher consumption of livestock products, better utilization and conservation of the soil and of feed supplies and by an increased industrial use of farm products.

The Latest Development: Facts Versus Propaganda

While the facts, as we hope to show convincingly in this report, are clearly developing in favor of lessening the controls over the food economy, the ideas seem still to run in the opposite direction.

Besides the propaganda of agencies, which almost by their nature are advocates of a continuation and even of a tightening of controls, such as the United Nations Relief and Rehabilitation Administration (UNRRA), the International Emergency Food Council (IEFC) and the FAO, and besides the measures taken by governments of food deficit areas, there have been added two remarkable actions accompanied by a special food scare propaganda. There are *bread rationing in Great Britain*, which started on July 21, and *bread rationing in South Africa*, which is to start on August 15.

Notes

1. FAO, Technical Supplement #4, Commodities, p. 8.

Chapter TWO

Building the Food Crisis into an International "New Deal"

Planning was Inevitable During the War

During the war and thereafter, the Combined Food Board (CFB), in which the United States, Great Britain and Canada were represented, had allocated the available supplies to the various countries. Its power of enforcement was enhanced by the fact that the same three nations governed the United Maritime Authority (successor to the International Shipping Pool). Allocations during the emergency of the first half of 1946 were thus made by the CFB; they were partly altered according to the recommendations of the Hoover Committee on May 12, 1946[1.]

The official international discussions of the food problems, however, are going on in the FAO. This is one of the suborganizations of the United Nations, but much closer to the actual decisions which are made in its field than most other committees of the United Nations. It has its seat in Washington. Its members and collaborators are partly the same as those of the CFB or its successor, the IEFC. There is close cooperation with the United States Department of Agriculture and the British and other nations' Food Ministries, and the FAO. The Chairman of the important meeting of the FAO, held May 20-27 in Washington, was Secretary of Agriculture, Clinton P. Anderson. The recommendations of the FAO, agreed upon together with some of the leading officials of the 21 member nations of the FAO, to which, however, the USSR does not belong, are therefore of great importance for international and national food policies.

The United Nations Relief and Rehabilitation Administration (UNRRA) played an influential part in the discussions of last spring, partly because it took care of those nations which suffered most from the crisis and for whom food had to be found, and partly because of the personality of its Director-General, former Mayor of New York City, Fiorello H. La Guardia.

The Psychological Crisis of February 1946

In order to get a clear understanding of the proposals made by the FAO and other regulating bodies to meet the crisis, it is necessary to understand the actual circumstances under which they were made.

The situation, which we outlined in Chapter I, and which became generally clear not before the beginning of February 1946, was certainly a psychological shock to all concerned. Besides the facts already quoted, there were the cries for help from India, which feared the repetition of the disastrous "Bengal famine" of 1943. Actual famine conditions existed in parts of the occupied territories, and even wealthy and normally well-provided countries like France, Holland, Belgium and Norway complained bitterly about severe food shortages.

This added greatly to the tendencies already adopted by many governments and their representatives in the FAO towards a rigid world-wide planned food economy, as perhaps most clearly revealed by the Australian delegate to the FAO when he said:

> As we handle these commodities through government collective channels, it is quite clear that we can subscribe to some of the fundamental desires of this Conference *that all commodities shall be channelled and regulated through government sources* ... In the final analysis, any campaign for increased food production rests on the shoulders of the individual producer; and because of that the individual producer is entitled to be assured that he will get fair remuneration for the effort that he puts into it.[2]

At the same meeting, the alternate delegate of the United Kingdom, Herbert Broadley, was equally clear:

> What it amounts to is that we need, really, the acceptance of a new system, of a new idea of proper responsibility, not merely the creation of new machineries. But new machinery is necessary . . .[3]

The Proposals of the FAO Meeting

While the United Nations' awareness of this crisis came too late to make very effective counter-measures possible for 1946, and it was the Hoover Committee which took over the task of ferreting out and redistributing the available supplies, the restrictive proposals made by the FAO were made as drastic as possible. They are a complete system. They involve restrictions on the distribution and utilization of grains, potatoes, peanuts and dried legumes, fats and sugars and dairy products, and the setting up of machinery to extend this control at least into the consumption year 1947/48.

For the 1946/47 consumption year, among other proposals made, were the following:

> The countries should consider the advantage of bread rationing.

> During the consumption year 1946/47 the use of grains for beverages and other non-essential purposes should be kept at the existing low levels and where possible should be further reduced.

> The use of edible potatoes for alcohol and other industrial purposes should be drastically curtailed and where possible prohibited.

For the 1947/48 consumption year the recommendations are as follows:

> Wartime controls should be re-established or maintained as long as shortages continue.

> Disorderly competitive buying by countries of foods in short supply is to be eliminated.

As long as shortages continue, such arrangements (purchasing the entire quantities of certain foods marketed)
should be maintained.

While the FAO is theoretically a policy-making organization
rather than a law-enforcing body, still the Committee recommends that where a country cannot follow the mentioned
"advices" of the Committee, its "government should report the
relevant circumstances to the IEFC and indicate what other
measures are being taken."

The FAO Committee while it expresses general approval of the
conclusion of a special memo submitted on May 20th, stated:[4]

that the world food shortage will continue to be acute at
least until the crops are harvested in 1947, and noted that
it does not estimate requirements or exportable surpluses
of individual countries, or make forecasts of effective
demand.

It therefore recommended:

That an international food, agriculture and fisheries
service be created to which should be entrusted the task
of preparing such appraisals . . .

The principal work of this FAO Research and Information Service, however, will be the making of definite
recommendations as to the "conservation and expansion
of supplies."

Is This In Fact a Plan for an Internationally Controlled Equalitarian Economy?

The significance of these proposals can be further clarified
when we examine the trend of thought which they represent.

Fiorello La Guardia, who now is the Director and dispenser of
the $3,500,000,000 fund of UNRRA, addressed the FAO on May
21, 1946. In the opening paragraph of his speech the real purposes
of these proposals are clearly and definitely stated:

If, out of this Conference, the world receives *a definite,
wonderful, concrete plan of operation for an international
controlled supervision of food production and the disposi-*

*tion of food, carrying out the ideals for which Sir John Orr
(Chairman of the FAO) has devoted his entire life* — if
that happens then the Security Council of the United
Nations at their bi-monthly meetings will be able to
spend most of their time on the golf links of Long Island.
And imagine, Mr. Gromyko then would be able to shoot
his hole-in-one to the admiration of the other players.

In discussing Herbert Hoover's suggestion at the same meeting
that the food and agricultural activities of UNRRA be absorbed
by a new UN Food Administration, and that it should be the
purpose of this Administration "to return to normal commerce
the food, fertilizer and farm supply business of the world with all
possible speed" and that "the world must quit charity as a basis
of widespread food distribution." Mr. La Guardia said:

> It is impossible to take a stopwatch and say on a given
> hour on a given day: "We are not going to give you any
> more food." *That is the old way.* I believe that there is a
> responsibility on the part of such nations who have food
> to see to it that countries that do not have food are fed
> until such time as they can get on their own feet.

To this we all agree and Herbert Hoover would be the first to
do so, but what Mr. La Guardia means by "until they get on their
own feet" is expressed in the next paragraph of his speech:

> Gentlemen, when I talk about "getting on their own
> feet," I mean just that in every sense of the word in the
> new world that we speak about. *To compel a starving
> nation to borrow on long terms for current food is not in
> keeping with the new world we are talking about...*

The World Food Bank

In discussing agricultural surpluses and deficit, which he be-
lieves should be handled by a "World Surplus Food Corporation" to insure parity price to all farmers throughout the world,
Mr. La Guardia said: "This organization could determine the
domestic requirements for each country for human consumption
and feeding. Mark you, I say requirements. I don't say the
amount that the purchasing power of the country could consume.

There is a big difference in many countries. Anything above that the producing country could declare surplus. Having declared that surplus, the regional corporation and the World Surplus Food Corporation would pool their surpluses, and ship it to countries, importing countries, each country to determine how the loss, if any, should be absorbed, the farmer, of course, being paid on a parity basis."

Mr. Hoover said: "Commerce will secure more economical distribution . . . I cannot too strongly emphasize that charitable distribution is hugely wasteful and inefficient."

Mr. La Guardia answered to Mr. Hoover's proposal: "I say it must be left to the United Nations Food Administration to determine the needs and methods of distribution."

In other words, Mr. La Guardia proposes an internationally controlled equalitarian economy under which the more efficient and prosperous nations will feed and support the less efficient and less prosperous nations, who will then "determine how the loss, if any, should be absorbed."

The International AAA

Let us see how the FAO now proposes to implement Mr. La Guardia's and Sir John Orr's "definite, wonderful, concrete plan of operation for an international controlled supervision of food production and the disposition of food":

The FAO Committee II in discussing the need of cooperation in food production said: "The Committee attaches importance to creating a feeling of confidence in regard to price stability (on the part of food producers)."

To achieve this end it finds that

> National guarantees of price stability need to be supplemented by international measures to serve the same end . . . The Committee therefore recommends that FAO be asked as a matter of urgency to study the problems of agricultural surpluses and the means which might be employed to dispose of them . . . To those assurances (regarding the problem of "eventual surpluses") the Committee wishes to add *assurance* concerning the returns received by agricultural producers *in all parts of the world.*

The Committee therefore recommends: "That FAO study the international aspects of the problems of securing reasonable and stable returns to agriculture in ways consistent with technological developments and a flexible world economy . . ."

Here we have in effect former Mayor La Guardia's proposal to create his World Surplus Food Corporation.

The FAO follows Mr. La Guardia's advice: "The Committee further recommends, while account should be taken of the desirability of maintaining or re-establishing normal trade between different countries, considerations of urgent need should be paramount — it is more important to provide food for starving people than to maintain or re-establish trade relations between different countries. Financial difficulties should not be allowed to hamper arrangements for providing food to countries in the most urgent need."

The ultimate aims of FAO were thus made to include objectives far beyond the range of the current crisis. What is proposed here is in effect the creation of an international agricultural "New Deal" operating under a controlled economy regulated either by the FAO or a similar body for an indefinite period.

Extending the Crisis

Sir John Orr, the Director-General of the FAO, feels certain that the shortage will last at least three years, and that world cooperation and planning will be necessary for the four to five years which it will take until the world food situation has become normal again.

The main report of the FAO meeting in Washington, released on June 6, 1946, contends that even if imports are kept high the urban food situation over wide areas in Continental Europe will again be disastrous in the spring of 1947 and that it will be impossible to help the Far East sufficiently.

In his desire to plan, the Director-General of the FAO has of necessity the support of those food deficit nations which do not expect to be able to pay for their imports in the immediate future. He also has the support of those countries which believe that a nationwide planning of the agricultural sector with guaranteed prices is necessary, for instance, Australia.

Britain's Bread Rationing

Britain's problem concerning shortages has been greatly emphasized by the introduction of bread rationing as of July 21. This measure in itself indicated that the British government considered lasting food shortages as being probable, as late as the end of June of this year. The British Labor government is sticking to rationing although it had to concede on July 17 to Winston Churchill that improved crops may make an early removal possible.

The repercussion of similar discussions in the United States was such that former cabinet members of our Administration again proposed the rationing of bread here — in spite of the constantly improving reports on crops from almost all parts of the world, and especially the United States; even editorials in the *New York Times* came out for bread rationing in this country.

Convinced that the present food emergency will continue for some considerable time . . . the FAO Committee therefore recommends: That there will be established an International Emergency Food Council . . . among whose functions will be: (a) to consider, investigate, inquire into and formulate plans with regard to any question in respect of which the member governments have, or may have, a common concern *relating to the supply and distribution in or to any part of the world, of foods, agricultural materials from which foods are derived, and equipment and non-food materials auxiliary to the production of such foods and agricultural materials,* and to make recommendations to the member governments in respect to any such question.

What Minimum Daily Calorie Requirement Must We Guarantee for the World?

The fact that the FAO is under the leadership and under the influence of nutritionists, may have an important bearing on the goals and perhaps even on the action of the United Nations. After an elaborate study on the normal and the minimum caloric intake, the FAO has established two minimum nutritional standards: one for an emergency period, and the other for an indefinite transition period. It seems to be its aim to secure these minimum calories for everyone.[5]

While an inter-allied committee for Germany had established a minimum standard of 1550 calories for the non-farm population, and the Hoover Committee applied for its emergency action "a 1500 - 1800 calorie bedrock figure"[1], the FAO declared that *an emergency subsistence level* for European nations should be at the minimum of 2200 calories at the retail level, which means a daily intake, on the average, of 1900 calories.

This level was accepted only for the period until the new harvest. After that time "a temporary maintenance level" of 2500 calories at the retail level, which would be equal to a 2200 calorie daily average intake, should be established.

For the Far Eastern countries the special committee of the FAO based its deliberations on an average food consumption of 2100 calories per capita per day on the retail level, which it assumed was actually consumed before the war. This is 12 to 20 percent less that consumed in the Western countries.

Starting from these levels, which as a whole have probably never been reached in the greater part of the Far East, the FAO committee came to the conclusion that the Far East alone, if the prewar level of consumption were to be achieved, would need imports of 25 million tons of rice in 1946, and if a fairly sufficient level were to be reached, at least 10 million tons of wheat or wheat equivalent would have to be sent to these countries. Nevertheless, the FAO decided at its general meeting that all import estimates should be based on a 1500-calorie intake.

How the members of the committee look at the actual state of things is very well illustrated by a number of tables in the special study on nutrition, the first technical supplement made for the conference of the FAO in May 1946. It gives four examples of how nutritional minimum standards should be reached by exports from the surplus states to the deficit states. The three deficit states are called "Faminaria, Starvania and Hungerland." The once called "Surplustate" is obviously the United States.[6]

To this the delegate for India at the FAO meeting on May 21 made this comment, which is as drastic as it is evidently ironical: "We first reduced our rations from 13 ounces (rice) per head to 9.6 ounces. This means 960 calories and this constitutes 80 percent of the diet . . . Consumption in some countries in the North American Continent, if reduced to calories in terms of cereal equivalent, would come to no less that 7000 calories per head."

The Views of Nutritionists Sometimes Seem Too Pessimistic

East of the Oder and Vistula a good part of the population were "involuntary vegetarians" throughout their lives. Measured by western caloric standards they should never have been able to become soldiers. However, they drove Hitler's armies from Stalingrad to the Elbe.

A personal experience: In 1918 and 1919, when this writer's husband was German Price Administrator and Under-Secretary for Commerce respectively, the most famous German nutritionists reproached the government because there was dangerous under-nourishment due to the impossibility of providing enough food. When he showed the statistics to them, which indicated that there was no visible increase in deaths from starvation, and that the infant mortality was almost normal, he was told that this was not the point. What mattered was that the youth of Germany was being crippled by insufficient diets. These were the same young people who, in 1940-45, fought the most violent war in mankind's history.

Now there is no question that there was serious malnutrition in the first part of this year, and that the infant mortality rate and the general death rate rose in some countries. But this does not mean that we have to assume that all people for whom we cannot provide 2500 calories per day are starving. Nearly all people in Berlin, except those with a good deal of money, were badly off until two months ago. At present, in June-July 1946, those who have some small plots of land — an many have — are doing much better. They write that they have new potatoes and vegetables, but to calculate their caloric intake would be difficult.

How the Actual Situation has Worked Out

In February 1946 the President asked former President Hoover to make a worldwide food survey. On May 13, after travelling 50,000 miles and visiting 25 different counties, Hoover stated: "At the time of our departure the Combined Food Board's estimate . . . showed a deficit as compared with stated requirements of 11 million tons cereal supplies. The gap in supplies between May 1st and September 30th can be reduced to about 3.6

million tons . . . In addition, there is a possible supply of about 1 1/2 million or more."

On June 29 Hoover reported in a broadcast from Canada with just pride "that this dangerous gap (of 3.6 million tons) had been closed."

The original estimate of the Combined Food Board was reduced in two ways; first, by scaling down the food requirements of the various deficit nations where they seemed too high; secondly, by reducing stockpiles — for instance, Great Britain — and diverting shipments destined for one country to another more in need of it; and thirdly, by getting larger deliveries from the surplus countries.

Not all surplus countries cooperated. Argentina, while making promises, has made only small deliveries, and is holding out for higher prices. Russia declined cooperation and restricted its help to the shipment of 11 million bushels of "election wheat" to France, and some small export to Finland.

World Government and National Food Policies

As long as we have no real world government, and as long as it is to the advantage of all that some nations show greater progress than others, it would be rather unwise to subject such vital far-reaching questions as the development of our food economy to the decision of others, many of whom already count very heavily on the somewhat overrated ability of the United States to pay unlimited sums.

These ideas are not confined to small segments of our politics; there are well known factions concerning these questions within the various agencies, and one party is clearly leaning towards world planning, the other sharply disinclined toward such ventures. It is not always easy to find out which of the two has been predominant in actual decisions of the administration, let alone which has had the upper hand in editing press releases.

The British Food Ministry can undoubtedly be considered to be strongly in favor of and influencing the FAO ideas.

The Fulfillment of the Aims of FAO Would be Dangerous to the United States

To try to improve and help the world in the way outlined by the Committee II of the FAO might entail such dangers for the United States as Mr. Bernard M. Baruch very frankly outlined in a letter to this writer's husband last fall, when he said: "I fear Europe will try to hang on to the United States and if we let them do that instead of making them do something for themselves, they will sink us too."

Even if the Untied States, as we anticipate, will not follow headlong a policy of unlimited charity, but rather go the way outlined by Hoover, the relatively large amount of loans which we are going to give might induce some nations to pursue the easy way of buying food instead of the more productive one of applying to the help of the United States to help themselves. We shall have to do our part to direct the money which we lend into productive channels.

The FAO Meeting of September 2

That the program for a planned world economy as outlined is actually to be proposed and acted upon at the forthcoming meeting of FAO in Denmark on September 2, 1946, is best witnessed by the closing remarks of Sir John Orr at the conference in Washington in May[8] "I believe we have surpassed our own intention. We have hammered out practical, concrete measures capable of immediate application to meet the continuing emergency of famine and scarcity. *At the same time we have initiated and endorsed the principle of long-term world food policy to meet all contingencies of world food supplies whether of deficiencies or surpluses.*"

The Bulletin closes as follows: "FAO plans to move up the date of the annual session of its Conference and has practically completed arrangements for opening the meeting in Copenhagen, Denmark of September 2nd. *At that time the Director-General will present his proposals for a permanent world food program.*"

Man-Made Shortages

Unequal Distribution

It would have been easier to overcome the worldwide food crisis if surpluses of one country could have been transferred to another country without haggling and without the medium of foreign exchange, and if those who had sufficient food would have shared with those of their compatriots who were starving. But this was not the case. In those countries where the need was greatest, such as Italy and Poland, the farmers were reluctant to sell their surplus grain, because they did not trust in the value of the money they were to receive, and for which at present they could not acquire the industrial goods they needed. This was understandable, but unfortunate.

All reports from France indicate that the farmers were living well, the big cities starved or lived from goods bought at excessive prices on the black market.

Spinach and other badly needed vegetables were reported to have been plowed under or to have rotted near Berlin in the spring of 1946, because the ceiling price did not make it worthwhile for farmers to sell.

In many war-torn countries the distribution of the available food, even of UNRRA food, functioned badly. We have only to think of China. The organization was best in Great Britain where the rationing system worked well, and the black markets played a minor role. (English newspapers even reported that the nutritional standards of the school children in the lower-paid income brackets were better than before the war because of the school lunches.)

The one commodity which was distributed to the countries, according to need when the emergency became evident, was bread grain. The CFB and the Hoover Committee saw to that as soon as the acuteness of the crisis was understood. But those foods which were more expensive did not move as easily. Free trade did not work as in happier days.

The Lack of Foreign Exchange

While we were having a surplus of eggs, the weary English housewives could not buy the powdered eggs which they received in gratifying amounts when Great Britain could purchase them on lend-lease account. The British contract for imports of powdered eggs from the United States was cancelled to save approximately $100 million a year in foreign exchange.

Just across the Dutch border, in the Ruhr, poorly fed German miners cannot be made to produce adequate quantities of coal, which the Western and Northern European industries need more than anything else. There is general agreement that the productivity of the Ruhr mines could be greatly increased if only more food, especially potatoes, were available. Unfortunately, exports from the British zone of Germany have to be paid for in dollars, since the English have to buy the grain for this zone from us. Consequently, the Dutch cannot exchange their potatoes and vegetables for coal, and the German miners do not get the available surplus of food, and the productivity of the miners is not increased. *The vegetables, in the meantime, had to be destroyed, as reported by visitors from Holland.*

The same happened with fish. In the midst of the crisis, nine out of ten Danish fishing boats were staying in port because they could not have sold their haul.'

A report from Sweden stated that in April that country's fishermen were throwing two-thirds of their catch back into the sea, because they could not sell it even at half price to Germany and Poland. The Norwegians likewise were unhappy that they could not export. Only later were arrangements made by the United States to export fish from the Scandinavian countries to Germany.

The Danes did not get permission from the CFB to sell their beef to Switzerland even though their warehouses were overflowing, and the farmers could not sell further beef cattle and had to feed it. It seems that the English wanted the beef, but at lower prices.

The Danes also had 50,000 horses which they wanted to sell. Draft power was badly needed all over Europe. Still the only horses which happened to be available could not be sold because the prices which the Danish farmers asked were too high. In June, 1946, an agreement was made, according to which the Danish government gave a donation to UNRRA, and UNRRA in turn used this amount to buy 10,000 horses at the farmers' price. What became of the 40,000 horses we don't know, but we do know that a horse eats 40% more grain feed than a dairy cow and that Denmark needs every ounce of grain to build up the dairy herds.

Another problem has been raised by the fact that some governments seem to make *distinction between hungry members of their own political faction and those of others.* It is reported from China that UNRRA supplies are reaching the Communist region at a rate of only one percent of the promised volume. Somewhat similar news comes from Greece and some areas behind the Iron Curtain.

Shall we finance and thereby maintain inefficiency in the distribution system of some countries?

Notes

1. Report of former President Hoover to President Truman on the Food Situation in Europe, U.S. Government Printing Office, Washington, 1946.
2. FAO Meeting, May 21, 1946, p.3.
3. FAO Meeting, May 21, 1946, p. 39.
4. FAO, "Appraisal of the World Food Situation 1946/47 and Related Documents" May 20, 1946.
5. Report on World Food Situation, Technical Supplement No. 2, *Nutrition* May 20, 1946.
6. Herbert Hoover, *World Famine Situation*, Address in Chicago, May 17, 1946.
7. FAO Report on World Food Situation, Technical Supplement No. 1 Nutrition, pp. 6-11 (mimeographed).
8. FAO Information Service Bulletin of June 6, 1946.
9. See the speech of the Danish delegate to the May Meeting of the FAO; also Politiken (Kopenhagen daily) and *Landbrugaadets Meddelelser*, American-Swedish News Exchange, Kooperatoeren.

Chapter THREE

The World's Food Supply

Wheat Production and Exports in the Four Main Exporting Countries
(Million bushels)

Country	Production			Net Exports
	Average 1935-39	1945	Average 1936-36 to 1939-40	1945-46
Argentina	222	148	121	60-70
Australia	170	130	100	40-50
Canada	312	306	181	355-365
United States	759	1,123	39	380
Total	1,463	1,707	441	835-865

The Great Grain Exporters

In times of emergency, breadstuffs are the most urgent of all needs.

It was only two of the four great wheat exporters, the United States and Canada, who liberated the world from the threatening mass catastrophe of famine in the spring of 1946. Argentina and

29

Australia, each of which in prewar times exported more than the United States, could make only relatively small contributions. The table on the opposite page tells the story of this performance.

Under the pressure of the threatened famine, two the four principal wheat exporters were able to deliver about double the volume of wheat which all four of them together had shipped in the average prewar year.

The prewar problem of each of these countries had been that of surpluses — and they all expected that one of their great problems very soon after the war would again be over-production. For this reason, and because wheat exports during the war decreased, three of them, Australia, Argentina and Canada, *had decreased their wheat acreages during the war.*

World wheat exports before the war averaged 625 million bushels. Wheat exporters besides the four mentioned above were Russia, Rumania, Hungary, Bulgaria, Yugoslavia, India and French North Africa. The two latter countries, which together exported on the average 28 million bushels, will probably not be able to resume their exports. Whether Russia will want to start shipments is improbable.

Of the four Danubian states, the most important one, Rumania, will be able to export wheat this year, and might send it to Central and Western Europe. It seems safe to assume that approximately 140 to 150 million bushels of wheat, which formerly came from other sources, will have to be supplied by Canada and the United States. In addition, these two countries will have to make up for lower production in Germany, Austria, some smaller European countries and in the Far East. The needed amounts are estimated in the previous chapter. But these export figures applied to a time when feed grains and potatoes were not used as breadstuffs as they are now. As the population in most wheat-consuming countries has not risen considerably since 1939, total consumption of wheat would be less than prior to the war, were it not for the fact that wheat at present has to compensate for the lack of fat, meat and other livestock products.

Feed Grains

For the problem of overcoming starvation, these exports do not give the whole picture. If needed, coarse grains can also help to feed human beings. Moreover, feed grains imports mean an immediate increase in livestock production for the importing countries.

Before the war, about 230 million bushels of corn were imported by Central and Western European countries, and more than 100 million bushels by Great Britain. A considerable part came from the Danubian countries, but the bulk of the world exports of corn were made by Argentina. In that country the fluctuations in the corn production were extremely heavy, production being between 358 million bushels and 104 million bushels a year in the thirties. Argentina will not be able to ship nearly as much as its prewar five-year average of 257 million bushels a year, but it might export 70 to 80 million bushels in the coming crop year. Considerable amounts of oats and even corn might be available from the United States.

In spite of the fact that the United States and Canada have exhausted their large carry-overs of wheat, the four exporting countries will probably be able to ship an even greater total amount of wheat and coarse grains than last year if needed, since Australia and Argentina have increased their wheat acreage and the United States and Canada are expecting bumper crops of wheat and feed grains. Curiously enough, *our own corn crop is one of the key factors for the world's wheat exports*. If no damage is done to the corn crop in August, it will be large enough to make wheat feeding above prewar levels unnecessary. This would allow for wheat exports of 300 million bushels without the need for too stringent government restrictions. It would also allow for the export of corn.

World corn exports will not be as high as in prewar times, nor will the same amounts be needed. A shift has occurred in that the North American countries have increased their livestock holdings and dairy production, and their exports of livestock products, and Argentina has increased its hog holdings and dairy production. On the other hand, in the whole of Europe the livestock population has decreased, and the traditional exports of meat, butter, eggs, etc. are on a very low level. Consequently, much more feed is needed in North America, Canada and Argentina, and less in Europe. Yet not nearly as much feed grain was exported to Great Britain and Continental Europe as was wanted by them.

There will be no sufficient substitutes for those vegetable oils and oilseeds which were imported by Great Britain and the Continental European countries from Asia. The United States, which lost its imports of copra and coconut oil from the Philippines, found substitutes in an increased soybean production, and is now able to export approximately 1 billion pounds of fats. The other increase in the production is that of sunflower seeds in Argentina, but even this will not suffice to supply Europe with its normal supply of fats and the oilcakes it fed its dairy herds.[1]

Canada

Canada, with a population of 11.5 million in 1933, was the world's greatest wheat exporter before the war. During the war, when wheat exports decreased, less wheat was grown, and a shift to greater livestock production occurred. Bacon and pork production in inspected slaughter-houses rose from a yearly average of 383 million pounds in 1935-39 to 746 million dozen to 379 million dozen during the same periods. Exports to Great Britain rose tremendously. In 1945-46 wheat growing was again on the uptrend, while the livestock population was on the decrease.

The new crop is estimated to be considerably larger, and may come nearer to the 490 million bushel 1939 record crop than any war crop. In 1939 the acreage planted with wheat was 27.8 million. This year, an acreage of 26.4 million is expected as against 23.4 million last year. No official crop estimates have been published so far, but in view of the excellent condition of the crop, private estimates come to "more than 400 million bushels."[2] The harvest will not start before the second half of August, and harm can still be done by bad weather. At present, an estimate of a 420 to 475 million bushel crop does not seem exaggerated. Five hundred million bushels have been mentioned by an "un-named official" of the USDA some weeks ago, which figure has been repeated by the *Corn Trade News*[3] but this figure seems too high, though not entirely impossible.

The carry-over of wheat will be 75 million bushels, which is considered low. Domestic consumption of wheat on the average of the years 1935-39 was 115 million bushels, but in 1945/46 it was close to 175 million bushels, because more wheat was fed to the increased livestock population. The combined fall and spring hog crop for 1945/46 is estimated at 15% less than a year ago, necessitating less feed in 1946/47, but cattle feeding is at high levels.

Since the oats, barley and mixed grain crops seems to be somewhat higher than last year, and the livestock holdings are lower, domestic disappearance of wheat might be lower than last year, probably between 140 and 165 million bushels. Exports of feed grains, which played a role in our own feed balance during the war, will scarcely be possible. Exports of wheat, however, might come up to 320 million bushels, though a somewhat lower figure, say 275 million bushels, is quite possible and 300 million bushels most likely, depending on the weather in the next weeks.

Pork Production and Exports

Besides wheat, Canada will send large amounts of bacon, ham, fresh beef, dairy products and eggs to Great Britain, while relief shipments of canned meat and dairy products to Belgium, Czechoslovakia, France, Greece and Poland may be continued if these countries still need them.

Canada's Production and Exports of Grain
(in million bushels)

	Wheat	Oats	Barley	Potatoes
Production				
Average 1935–39	312	338	89	64
1945/46	306	382	158	60
1946/47*	420–475	400–410	160	74
Domestic Disappearance				
Average 1935–39	115	320	39	39
1945/46	175	425	42	72
1946/47*	140–165	395–405	160	74
Net Export				
Average 1935–39	180	8	14	−5
1945/46	350	15	—	−10
1946/47	275–320	5	—	—

*estimate

Great Britain's Wheat Provider For Four Years

Canada has just negotiated a four-year wheat contract with Great Britain providing for the sale of 160,000 bushels of Canadian wheat at $1.55 a bushel for each of the two crop years 1946/47 and 1947/48; 140,000 bushels at not less than $1.25 a bushel in 1948/49, and 140,000 bushels at not less than $1.00 in 1949/50. This deal, which was under discussion for some months, was objected to by the American as being against the spirit of multilateral free trade. Consequently, it has been provided for that the terms of the deal:

> Shall be subject to any modification of amendment that may be necessary to bring it into conformity with any international agreement or arrangement hereafter entered into to which both governments are parties.[4]

The new trade agreement is very beneficial to Canada since it assures it of a market for its main export commodity at a time when it will again be freely available and probably in abundance. It is, of course, detrimental to the United States, since Great Britain imported as much as one-third of the wheat which moved in the world market before the war, and we will soon be looking for export outlets for our wheat. The price of $1.55 a bushel is below the prevailing market price, but might be the normal price in a few months. Canada has therefore provided nicely for itself, and we are not surprised that Senator Wherry of the wheat-raising state of Nebraska is complaining bitterly.

Argentina

When Wheat Became Fuel

Before the war, Argentina was the world's greatest exporter of corn, linseed and meat, and the second greatest exporter of wheat. During the war, due to lower demand, Argentina decreased its wheat and corn acreage, but increased tremendously — partly on the instigation of the United States — the output of sunflower seed and also that of livestock products such as pork, eggs and dairy products. Surpluses of grain were accumulated during the war in spite of lower acreage. Corn and linseed were used as fuel, wheat deteriorated in storage. Prices for these commodities during the war were very low.

Government Makes Good Profits,
Even in an Emergency

The data about the 1945/46 harvest, which was harvested last winter, are not satisfactory. The wheat crop seems to be 143.5 million bushels. Prices for grain have been raised and the government has a monopoly on wheat, corn and sunflower seed purchases, reselling to foreign countries at much higher prices than paid to the farmers.

The exports both of wheat and of corn have turned out to be below estimates, and below the promises made. Wheat exports amounted from July through December 1945 to approximately 34 million bushels, and from January until June 10 of this year to about 30 million bushels. They went principally to countries which could pay well for them, such as Brazil and other Latin American countries, Belgium and Portugal. Some gift exports were made to France, Italy and to UNRRA for shipments mainly to China.

Wheat exports in the second half of 1946 are expected to be 37 to 38 million bushels, more than in the same period last year, but much below prewar. In the first half of 1947, when the new crop is being marketed, exports should be greater than the same period of this year, since the wheat acreage is being increased.

Corn production in 1945/46 was only 57% of average. Exports were low. Also in 1947 the corn acreage will be below normal. The sunflowerseed crop, estimated at 2,208 pounds will be expected at excellent prices.

Argentina is evidently *holding out for higher prices*. Its good will in helping to overcome the food crisis can be considered as negligible. Only recently, 161 ships were reported to be in its ports; none of them could get a permit to leave the country.

Since the acreage planted for wheat and corn will be much larger this year, exports of 100 million bushels of wheat can be expected, and corn exports might be larger than in 1945/46 if the weather is good to fair. As soon as it is evident that the world need for wheat is less than expected and prices threaten to turn downward, wheat can be expected to move at an accelerated rate. At present, Argentina is trying to force the United States to sell it trucks and tires by claiming that the crops cannot be moved to the ports due to the lack of transportation. There might be some truth in this and exports may accelerate, if and when tires and trucks arrive.[5]

Australia

Australia, with 7.125 million people, is self-sufficient in regard to almost all foods. In addition, it is normally an important surplus producer of grains, sugar, meat, dairy products and fruit. During the war, Australia provided the Allied Military services in the Pacific with large amounts of fresh food. From 1943 to the mid-summer of 1945 it experienced a severe drought which reduced food production to two-thirds of normal and decreased the sheep flocks.

Prior to the war, Australia produced between 155 and 170 million bushels of wheat on 13 million acres. Approximately 100 million bushels were exported. The 1945/46 wheat crop was estimated at 135 million bushels from a much lower acreage, namely 11.5 million acres. This year the goal has been raised to 15.5 million acres, which would be nearly 20% higher than in prewar times. Whether this goal can be reached will depend on the weather until the end of the planting time. There is a shortage of tractors, machine parts and labor, while the fertilizer situation has already improved. Even if the goal of 15.5 million acres should not be reached, which seems possible, wheat exports of 100 to 110 million bushels equal to those prior to the war, if not larger, can be hoped for. No exports of feed grains can be expected, but sugar exports will rise to about prewar levels.

During the war, Australia increased her production of butter, cheese, bacon and pork, and exports of these commodities will be larger in 1946/47 than in prewar times. It is hoped that the shipping space available will make it possible to begin exports of fruits again.[6]

The United States

The Grain-Livestock Ratio of 1946/47

This crop year will find us in a much better grain position than the year 1945/46, barring damage to the corn crop in August. Despite lower carry-overs of wheat and corn, a somewhat larger aggregate amount of wheat, corn and oats will be at our disposal than was last year, while the export demand for wheat will be smaller. There will be approximately 180 to 200 million bushels less of wheat, but 200 to 300 million bushels more of our most valuable feed grain, corn, and the quality of the corn can be expected to be considerably better than last year when part of it was soft or wet. The supply of oats will be somewhat larger because of the higher carry-over.

Demand and Supply of Feed Grains

There will be more feed grains available than in any previous year because of the expected record corn and oat crops, while the demand for feed will be considerably lower than in 1942/43 and 1943/44 and less than in 1945/46 due to the smaller number of

---

Grain Supplies in the United States
1945/46 and 1946/47

(in million bushels)

		1945/46	1946/47*
Wheat	carry-over	280	100
	new production	1,123	1,132
		1,403	1,232
Corn	carry-over	311	200
	new production	3,078	3,490
		3,389	3,690
Oats	carry-over	220	320
	new production	1,546	1,471
		1,768	1,791
Barley	carry-over	70	70
	new production	277	230
		347	300
Number of grain-consuming animal units on January 1st		146,600,000 (1946)	138,000,000–140,000,000 (1947)

---

*estimate

Wheat Distribution & Supply
1944–1947*

1600

1400

1944–1945	1945–1946	1946–1947
Carry Over 281	Carry Over 108	Reserve for Other Use
Industrial 96	Industrial 96	Carry Over ?#
Export 139	Export 390	Export 250
Seed 80	Seed 82	Seed 85
Feed 282	Feed 328	Feed 150
Food 559	Food 475	Food 450

1200

1000

800

600

400

200

1944–1945   1945–1946   1946–1947

---

*1946–1947 figures correspond to preliminary allocations of the Dept. of Agriculture.

Source: U.S. Department of Agriculture

animals to be fed in the first nine months of the crop year. The decrease until then will mainly be in hogs.

The fall pig crop is expected to be only 29 million as against 35 million in 1945 and 47.7 million in 1939. The spring pig crop, however, may be considerably larger than in each of the two past years, when it was 52 million, making for an increase in demand for feed in the last months of the crop year. The number of cattle will probably be somewhat lower than last year, while there will again be fewer horses. The number of chickens and turkeys will depend on the amount of meat available over the crop year, but the number of chickens is conservatively estimated to be on 20 to 25 million less on January 1, 1947 than at the same time in 1945/46.

Wheat

Since more corn will be available than in the previous year, while the demand for feed will be somewhat less, less wheat will be fed to animals even without stringent government restrictions. In 1945/46, 328 million bushels of wheat were fed as against 282 million bushels in 1944/45, and 122 million bushels in 1940/41. Two hundred million bushels of wheat to be used for feed in 1946/47 seems a good estimate; it depends partly on how much wheat will be used in feed mixtures.

Exports of wheat scheduled from this country are set at 50 million bushels. Subtracting 30 million bushels which the government is holding for exports from its 1945/46 purchases, this means only 220 million bushels from the new harvest. Promises of the amount were made in May when the wheat harvest was estimated at one billion bushels as against the new estimate of 1.132 billion bushels on July 22, 1946. Feeding of wheat was to be scaled down to 150 million bushels, whereas we figure on 200 million, since this figure, while coming up to the actual demand, will not weigh down our wheat balance for 1946/47 too heavily. We assume that the higher wheat extraction rate will be kept up because there were scarcely any complaints from the public.

Our wheat balance will then look as follows:

Wheat Distribution and Supply
1945/46 and 1946/47

	1945/46	1946/47
Food	475	450
Feed	328	200
Seed	82	85
Exports	390	220
Industrial Use	20	—
Total	1,295	955
Supply*	1,403	1,232
Carry-over and use for purposes not yet specified	100–08	277

*see previous table

This would allow for an increase of our carry-over of wheat of approximately 100 million to 200 million bushels. Since so high a carry-over is not necessary, 25 to 50 million bushels more can easily be diverted to additional exports if needed, or used for any other purpose. Restrictions on the use of wheat can be eased.

In addition, we shall be able to export oats. The supply of oats for the 1946/47 crop year will be 1.79 billion bushels, consisting of 1.47 billion bushels from the new crop and a carry-over of 300 to 320 million bushels. Not more than 1.45 billion bushels has ever been used for all purposes in one crop year, but even this much will hardly be needed if the corn harvest comes up to expectations. Allowing for a carry-over of 150 million bushels, 200 million should therefore be available for export. Since this is too much for use as food, oats available for feed in Europe can be shipped, if the price is not too high. This will make it possible for some European countries, notably Holland and Denmark, to increase their cattle and hog holdings. Probably also considerable quantities of corn for exports will be available.

What If Bad Weather Should
Damage the Corn Crop?

This picture would look different if, because of unfavorable weather in August, the corn crop did not come up to expectations. In this case, the 1947 spring pig crop would probably not be higher than in the past two years, the poultry flocks would be brought down to meet the actual demand and animals generally would be fed to lower weights than in the past crop year. Exports of corn would not be possible, but because the number of animals will be lower than previously, and food wheat and oat crops are assured, there would be no difficulty exporting the promised amount of wheat and 100 million bushels of oats, and ease the restrictions on the domestic use of grains.

Feed is the Decisive Factor in Our Food Supply

Our Livestock and Feed — The Central Problem
for the United States in 1946/47

The question of whether our crops will be sufficient for consumption and export in any crop year has always been largely a question of how great our livestock holdings were. *Livestock consumes infinitely more grain than human beings do.* Mr. A.P. Jacobsen, Danish delegate to the FAO, stated at the meeting on May 20 in Washington:

> Two or three persons can live on the grain needed to feed one hog, and one person can live on the grain for seven hens. The loss of calories in the feeding of hogs amounts to 80% and in the feeding of chickens to 90%.

Two-Thirds to Three-Quarters of the
Nation's Land is Used for Animals

In the United States, between 65 and 70 million acres of land were cultivated during the war for wheat, but as many as 165 million acres for the four feed grains — corn, oats, barley and grain sorghum. Of these latter, 85% were used for feed, and in addition, between 115 and 487 million bushels of wheat — up to half of the total harvest. And this does not include the acreage used for hay and pasture, which amounts to more than 50% of the total farm land, nor does it include other kinds of feed, such as oil-cakes and meal, and animal protein feeds such as molasses.

Ratio of Feed to Livestock Upset During the War

At the beginning of the war it became imperative to increase our supply of such concentrated foods as milk, fats, meats and eggs. The method used to accomplish this was to raise prices so as to make the ratio between feed and livestock products attractive. The outcome was that the production of livestock rose by 39% during the war.

At the same time, the output of feed, that is feed grains and hay, rose by only 24%. This 15% discrepancy, due to the greater increase of livestock products, was possible only because of the enormous carry-over of wheat and feed grains with which we started the war — a remainder of the prewar surpluses — and which has by now been brought down to a minimum. The feed deficit was partly compensated by the continuous decrease of horses and mules. These decreased from January 1, 1940 to January 1, 1946 from 14.1 million to 11.5 million, that is by approximately 2.6 million, or sufficient to save enough grain to feed 3.64 million dairy cows per year.

Increasing the Feed Yield Per Acre

The crop land used for grains was scarcely increased during the war. *The additional feed which was produced was the result of higher yield per acre.* This was made possible by the use of *new improved varieties of seed*, by a *greater application of chemical fertilizer per acre*, by a shift in hay crops and by the use of more machinery. All these trends are continuing and are bound either to increase our grain supply or decrease the acreage used for crops. High-yielding hybrid corn in now being used widely, but not yet as much as it could be, and the new strains of oats have only recently been introduced.[7] The rising demand for chemical fertilizers,[8] which it was never possible to satisfy during the war, is still very much on the increase, and there is a huge backlog in demand for agricultural machines, tractors and equipment. Pasture is being shifted to higher-yielding grass, and grass hay is steadily being replaced by legume hays with a higher feed value.

Corn is by far our main feed crop. Until recently, it made up 73% of the feed grains which were marketed, while oats, which were mostly used on the farms, amounted to only 17%, barley to

Total Cropland, and Crop Production Per Acre, United States, 1919–45

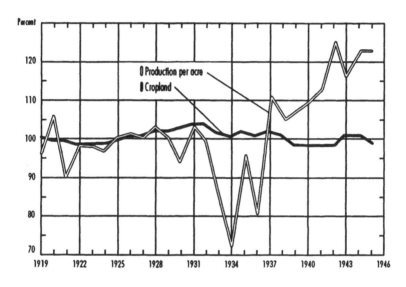

Data for 1944 and 1945 are preliminary.

*Total cropland is the sum of the estimated acreage of land from which one or more crops were harvested plus estimated crop failure and summer fallow acreage.

Source: U.S Department of Agriculture.

7% and grain sorghum to 2%. This ratio is bound to change somewhat, however, since the yield of oats is rising, and for soil conservation purposes some of the corn acreage will be shifted to a rotation of legume hays and oats.

Manipulating the Corn-Hog Ratio

Because of the preponderance of corn, approximately 50% of the hogs and 80% of the so-called feeder cattle are raised in the five states of the Corn Belt (Ohio, Indiana, Illinois, Iowa and

Missouri). The Corn Belt is also the Hog Belt, and the number of hogs is closely correlated to the corn crops. A good corn harvest means a good pig crop in the following year. This may be changed only if the government, by purposely fixing the prices of corn and of hogs, attempts to alter the natural price relationships.

Not only the number, but also the weight at which hogs are slaughtered is decided by the corn-hog ratio, that is by the number of bushels of corn for which one hog can be bought. A sudden drop in this ratio means a certain run of hogs to the slaughterhouses. This happened in the summer of 1944, when the support price for hogs was suddenly decreased. That did not happen. As the government hoped it would, in May and June of this year, when feed prices were suddenly increased and meat prices kept stable. At that time the ceiling price was no longer the real price, the corn-hog ratio being already dependent on the black market price for hogs, and on confidence that hog prices would eventually have to be raised to meet the price of corn.

The Feed-Consuming Capacity of Our Livestock

Just as corn is the main feed crop, so *hogs consume most of the feed grains*, even though a single hog uses less than a dairy cow. Before the war, hogs used up 37% of all feed grains, but due to the fact that hogs reproduce quickly, and an increase in meat was called for, they increased their share to 40%.

Next in importance for our feed grain supply are chickens and turkeys, which have also been responsible for the disappearance of a goodly amount of wheat. Dairy cattle, whose diet is supplemented by large amounts of other concentrated feeds and of hay and pasture, are only third in importance as consumers of feed grains. The share of horses and mules is continually decreasing, and at present is lower than that of beef cattle which are fourth. The grain consumption of sheep and lambs is negligible.

Expressed in terms of grain consumption, pork, chickens and eggs seem to be our most costly form of protein food. Hogs and poultry were chiefly responsible for the shortage of feed, which occurred every spring from 1943 on.

U.S Corn Production
(in billion bushels)
vs.
Grain-Consuming Animal Units
(in million head)

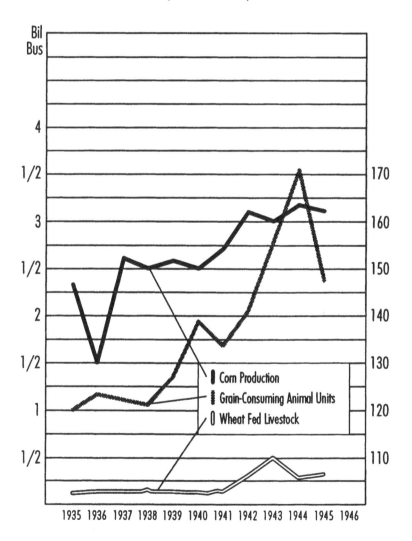

The same amount of grain, approximately 0.715 tons (27.4 bushels) is needed to produce:[9]

1. 4,237 pounds of milk
2. 3,704 pounds of lamb
3. 853 pounds of beef cattle
4. 314 pounds of hogs (liveweight)
5. 185 dozen eggs
6. 70 chickens
7. 20 turkeys
8. or to feed 0.695 horses a year

The livestock and poultry on farms must therefore be considered not only as existing food supply, but as *feed-consuming liability on our animal agricultural balance sheet.*

To see this more clearly, it is expedient to express the number of the various animals as "grain-consuming animal units"[10] as a common denominator for the probable use of feed grain. A dairy cow under this concept is considered one unit. A horse or a mule, which consumes 1.4 times as much as one dairy cow per year, equals 1.4, a hog 0.87 units, one beef animal 0.51 units, one sheep .04 units, and one chicken 0.045 units. Grain-consuming animal units increased as follows over the war years:[11]

Grain Consuming Animal Units, January 1

(in thousand units)

1939	127.0
1940	118.5
1941	133.4
1942	143.1
1943	159.6
1944	171.1
1945	146.2
1946	146.6

Note that the peak year was 1944, or rather the 1943/44 crop year. The small increase in 1946 is due to an increase of hogs and chickens on January 1, 1946, over the year before. At the same time the number of cattle and horses had decreased.

It would be simpler if we could simply multiply the number of animal units by a specified amount consumed by one animal unit per year. This would be possible if the animals were, on average, fed to the same weights, and if the quality of the grain were uniform over the years. But this is far from being the case. The amount of grain fed varies with the demand for meat, the quality of corn and the price ratio between livestock products and feed. During the war the use of feed grains per animal unit (corn, oats and barley) increased considerably. It reached its peak in the first half (October-March) of the 1945/46 crop year, partly because livestock and poultry were fed heavier than ever before, but also because of the lower quality of the corn in some main producing areas.

As a consequence, hogs marketed in early 1946 averaged about 20 pounds heavier than a year earlier, and heavier than any year on record. A larger-than-usual proportion of steers slaughtered were of high quality, reflecting higher feeding. Egg production per laying hen was at the highest rate we ever had. Even the average weight of turkeys was above any previous year.

While the above figures hold well generally, it should not be forgotten that the law of diminishing returns is valid for livestock production, too. From a certain point on, additional feed units give lower relative yields in meat, milk or eggs. This is one reason why the USDA tried to discourage the feeding of hogs to high weights, when the sudden need for large grain exports arose this spring.

A recent interesting study comes to the conclusion that:[12] "The point of greatest efficiency, measured by points of edible body nutrients, occurs for 2-year old steers just before average Good slaughter grade is reached; for the yearlings just beyond average Good slaughter grade."

Since, according to the author, "The food grade slaughter animal contains about as much fat as the average individual will consume along with the lean."[13] he thinks that it would be good policy, in times of food scarcity, to fatten choice feeder steer calves only to Good slaughter grade. "The feed used annually to fatten cattle in the Corn Belt beyond average Good slaughter grade during the period 1938/39 to 1941/42 would have been sufficient to fatten an additional 1.7 million head."[14]

But in spite of lower yields per additional feed unit, such heavy feeding will take place whenever the hog-feed price ratio, or the higher price for highly fed cattle it still leaves a profit.

How Much Feed Will We Need in 1946/47?

During part of each of the past three seasons there was a shortage of feed in spite of the highly increased production of feed. Imports of oats and barley from Canada became necessary, and the Commodity Credit Corporation (CCC) sold wheat from their surpluses to feeders. The reason was the high demand for livestock products, and to a minor degree, the fact that relatively little grain is sold from the farms between March and June, and that an increasing number of animals were fed in establishments which had to buy feed.

As a comparison, the tables below show the number of livestock and the feed which was available for them in the years 1939-46.

Most striking in these two tables is the tremendous increase in corn production. Nearly as astonishing is the corresponding increase in the pig crop which reached its peak of 121.7 million heads in 1943, following the record corn crop of 1942. In spite of the large corn supplies, 486 million bushels of wheat, which were held by the CCC, were fed, in addition to feed grains in 1943/44.

Reduction of the Hog Population in 1944

In the spring and summer of 1944, when the 1943 pig crop, which was farrowed early in 1943, came to market, the supply of pork became greater than the demand. Rationing was abolished for seven months, and pork flooded the market. For the first time since the drought years, there was a definite scarcity of feed during the 1943/44 crop year, and as a result a much lower pig crop in the fall of 1944 and in the spring of 1945. With no great feed reserves to draw on, the 1945 hog crop was only 86.8 million head, which was as low as in 1939, and only somewhat more than in the pre-drought years, when the corn crop was one-fifth to one-third lower. Yet, because of heavy feeding of the animals, there was no oversupply of feed.

Livestock on Farms, January 1, 1939 to January 1, 1946
(in million head)

Year	Horses and Mules	All Cattle	Hogs	Pig Crop Calendar Year	Sheep	Chickens
1939	14.8	66.0	50.0	87.0	51.6	418.6
1940	14.5	68.2	61.1	79.8	52.4	438.3
1941	14.1	71.5	54.3	84.7	54.3	422.9
1942	13.7	75.2	60.4	104.6	56.7	474.9
1943	13.4	79.1	73.7	121.7	55.8	540.8
1944	12.8	82.4	83.9	86.8	51.8	576.4
1945	12.3	81.9	59.8	87.0	47.8	510.9
1946	11.6	79.8	62.3	18.0*	44.2	525.5

Production of Feed Grains and Wheat Used as Feed, 1939/40–1945/46
(in million bushels)

Year	Corn	Oats	Barley	Wheat Fed
1939/40	2,581	958	278	115
1940/41	2,462	1,245	309	122
1941/42	2,676	1,181	362	116
1942/43	3,132	1,350	429	292
1943/44	3,034	1,138	324	486
1944/45	3,228	1,166	284	281
1945/46	3,018	1,547	263	382
1946/47*	3,489	1,471	230	200

* estimate

Due to the low pig crop of only 29 million, which is expected in the fall, the pig crop of calendar 1946 will probably be six million less than in 1945, and the lowest since 1938.

The Cattle Situation

The increase in cattle over the war years has been more moderate than would be expected. The number of cattle reached its peak at the beginning of 1944, when it was 82.3 million heads as against 66 million in January 1939, and decreased to 79.8 million at the beginning of this year. This increase was one of beef cattle. The number of dairy cattle was mainly only two million heads higher at the beginning of this year than in 1939.

Of special interest for the demand for feed grains is that part of the beef cattle which each year is sold from the ranches to the feeders, mostly in the Corn Belt, to be grainfed. *Grainfed cattle normally accounts for about one-third of the beef supply*, excluding veal, and its share in the grain consumed by beef cattle is paramount. The number of cattle on feed lots was 3,303,000 at the beginning of 1937, and 4,157,000 in January of this year, which is somewhat lower than last year. Since then it has declined due to the tight feed situation and was 17% lower on April 1 of this year than last.

A relatively narrow spread between prices of feeder and of fed cattle existed since last year, which made grain feeding unprofitable. The release of meat from Office of Price Administration (OPA) ceilings, and a record corn crop, might reverse this situation completely, especially if there should be a ceiling on grain prices but not on meat.

The Poultry Population

The number of chickens was 419 million at the beginning of 1939, and reached its peak on January 1, 1944, when it was 577 million. At the beginning of this year it was still 520 million, which is too high for the prevailing demand, since takings of eggs, chickens and turkeys by the military are comparatively low. Eggs, consequently, have become surplus goods, and the warehouses were overflowing with eggs and poultry even when red meat was very scarce in early summer. With more meat available, the demand for chicken and eggs was already decreasing in the middle of July. Larger exports of eggs are hoped for. But eggs are difficult to transport overseas, and the spoilage is high. Those foreign countries which import our eggs would much rather import feed grain and build up their own poultry flocks. A decrease of our chicken flocks is definitely warranted from the standpoint of the economy, and because of the supply-demand situation.

Summary

Feed Demand in 1946/47

The feed demand in the new crop year will probably be lower than in 1945.

The number of hogs to be fed will be smaller over the first nine months, since the fall pig crop will be smaller than last year. It is true that the next spring crop of hogs will be larger than in 1946, if the corn crop turns out as well as expected, but this possible increase would make itself felt only during a few months of the crop year. It is expected that hogs will not be fed to such excessive weights as in 1945/46, because the hog-corn ratio might not be as advantageous under a free price system.

The number of cattle is expected to decrease somewhat. High feeding, however, is possible, especially if no ceiling price is put on meat; it is certain, if only grain has ceiling prices and livestock prices are left free.

Poultry flocks are expected to decrease somewhat, depending on the price of corn. Eggs have to be supported at rather high levels by the government, and their production will therefore not follow the law of demand and supply.

On January 1, 1945, we had 146.2 million grain-consuming animal units, including chickens, and 0.4 million more on January 1, 1946. This was considerably less than in 1944. On January 1, 1947, the number of animal units may be 140 million, or at least 6.6 million less than on January 1, 1945. According to a rough estimate there will be a decrease of

600,000	horses	.84	million animal units		
500,000	dairy cattle	.50	"	"	"
1,000,000	beef cattle	.50	"	"	"
6,000,000	hogs	5.22	"	"	"
20 - 25,000,000	chickens	.90	"	"	"

7.96 million animal units

Feed Supply

We have tried to compare the feed supply of the new crop year with that of the last years. This year we will have no reserve of corn to draw on, but we have had little in the last two years. There will be no imports of oats and barley. Certainly, the amount of wheat to be fed will be lower than in any of the war years. Since the carry-over of wheat is exceedingly small and exports will continue, even if the wheat crop is 1.132 billion bushels, only 200 million bushels of wheat can be fed (as compared with the 150 million allocated for this purpose by the USDA). These 200 million bushels would be 128 million less than last year, and 287 million less than in 1943.44. Probably there will not be any demand for more wheat for feed purposes.

As the *corn situation* looks now, we shall have the largest crop on record. Government estimates go as high as 3.5 billion bushels, 400 to 450 million more than last year, and 250 million more than the record crop of 1942. This will make for a sufficient amount of corn to be marketed. Of course, the weather in August can do much to reduce this figure.

There is no uncertainty, though, about the *oat crop*. It will again be nearly 1.5 billion bushels, which is more than was used this year. This comes on top of a sizable carry-over of oats from the 1945/46 crop, which will not nearly be used on the farms. The high corn and oat crops together will mean more feed grains to be sold from the farms, and the possibility that the chronic shortage of commercial grains in the spring will be avoided next year.

If the estimate of a 3.5 billion bushel corn crop comes true, *we will have a larger supply of feed than in any prior year*, including the years 1942/43 and 1943/44, while the number of grain-consuming animal units will be smaller than in any war year except 1941/42, and as much as 21% smaller than in 1942/43.

Even if the 1947 spring pig crop should be greater than the 1946 spring pig crop, and even if feeding remains fairly high, the feed supply in the crop year 1946/47 should be ample. A tight situation could only come about if grains, but not livestock, were to have ceiling prices applied to them. In any case, exports of oats for human consumption, as well as for feed, should become possible. Even if the corn crop should turn out somewhat smaller than expected, the grain supply should be sufficient because of the lower number of animals.

Notes

1. See the section on Fats and Oils (p. 118.)
2. Foreign Crops and Markets, Vol. 52, No. 29.
3. Published by *Broomhall's International Grain Statistics*, July 25, 1946.
4. See *New York Times*, July 26, 1946.
5. Material for the section on Argentina taken from: The First National Bank of Boston: The Situation in Argentina, July 1945 through June 1946 editions; *Buenos Aires Weekly*: "The Review of the River Plate"; U.S. Department of Agriculture: "Foreign Crop Markets"; personal information.
6. Material for Australia taken from: U.S. Department of Agriculture: "World Food Situation, 1946"; U.S. Department of Agriculture Foreign Crops and Markets Reports; and *Neue Züricher Zeitung*.
7. See Appendix 3.
8. See Appendix.
9. U.S. Department of Agriculture, *Feed Grains and Meat Animals*, p. 48.
10. U.S. Department of Agriculture, *Agricultural Statistics*, p. 339.
11. U.S. Department of Agriculture, *Agricultural Statistics*, p. 339.
12. Aaron S. Nelson, "Input-Output Relationships in Fattening Calves," *Journal of Farm Economics*, May 1946.
13. ibid.
14. ibid.

Chapter **FOUR**

The World Demand for Food

Continental Europe

The Probable Size of Requirements for Continental Europe 1946/47

At the beginning of May the FAO estimated the food "deficit" of Continental Europe, which has to be made up by imports of wheat, other grains for feed and dry legumes, at 12.5 million tons.[1] This estimate was based on April crop reports and was made at a time when the actual food situation in many European countries was as bad as could be. Since then favorable news has come from most of Europe, favorable both as to the weather, the size of the crop, and to the return to normal conditions generally. The lack of fertilizer, which was considered a serious handicap in some countries, did not weigh as heavily as had been feared; in others, enough fertilizer had been provided for. In most countries the soil has been fully cultivated, contrary to expectations. Not only grain crops over the whole of Western and Southern Europe have turned out very well—though still somewhat under normal prewar standards—but the sugar crops have also improved and so has the output of olives, which is so important for the Mediterranean countries. Much higher than prewar potato crops are expected.

In mid-June, when the full impact of the improvement was not yet visible, the Office of Foreign Agricultural Relations (OFAR), which is collaborating with the FAO, *reduced the "requirement" for wheat imports* (including other grains for food and dry legumes) *from 12.5 million tons to 10 million tons*, if three-quarters of a million short tons each of pure fat, sugar and meat (including fish) and some dairy products can be imported.[2]

At the same time the number of calories per day per person has tacitly been increased somewhat to 2,300 for the non-farm population generally, and in no country to less than 2,000. These amounts are for Germany considerably higher than those considered by the occupation authorities for the emergency (actually 1550 calories), and than the 1500–1800 calories which were used as the basis of Mr. Hoover's calculations last spring.

OFAR, after stating the above figures of requirements, adds that these quantities of wheat, meat, fat and sugar will "not necessarily be asked for nor supplied."

Seven to eight hundred thousand tons of meat imports can evidently be counted upon, since the U.S. Bureau of Agricultural Economics in its July issue of *The Livestock and Wool Situation* estimated that meat imports into Continental Europe will amount to at least that much. In addition, very large imports of fish from Scandinavia are possible and partly scheduled. Because of the increased sugar production in Cuba and the Caribbean, sugar imports will probably also come up to the standards of the OFAR. There will be substantial imports of oils and fats, but in addition we expect an increase in the indigenous fat production as a consequence of imports of feed grains. It should be kept in mind, however, *that imports of these more expensive foodstuffs will not be distributed over the whole of Europe.* The Eastern Countries, Greece and Italy, will hardly import any meat after the end of the relief shipments of the UNRRA late this year.

An additional intake of calories will, in some countries, be provided through *alcoholic beverages,* wine and beer. Good grape crops are reported from France, Spain and Italy. The FAO report of May 20th states explicitly that not included in its minimum intake are alcoholic beverages, which in prewar times accounted to about 400 calories per capita per day in France, 200 in Italy, Switzerland, Portugal, Spain and Belgium, and in other countries about 100. These intakes, according to the FAO, may not re-approach their prewar levels in Germany and Austria.

Food and Feed Net Trade of Groups of Countries in Greater Europe, Average 1934–38

(thousand metric tons)

Food or Feed	British Isles	Total Continental Importers	Eastern Exporters*	Soviet Russia
Wheat grain	+ 5,465	+ 4,724	− 1,289	− 586
Rye grain	+ 6	+ 738	− 401	− 162
Rice	+ 119	+ 946	+ 109	+ 37
Wheat and rye flour	+ 340	− 123	− 183	− 43
Dried beans	+ 43	+ 135	− 131	− 16
Sugar	+ 1,889	+ 503	− 96	− 105
Major fruits	+ 1,435	+ 379	+ 10	+ 17
Meat	+ 1,372	− 119	− 71	0
Eggs	+ 194	− 5	− 74	0
Cheese	+ 141	− 55	− 5	0
Processed milk	+ 82	− 204	0	0
Butter	+ 459	− 156	− 12	− 21
Vegetable oils	+ 128	− 43	− 1	− 7
Whale oil, lard	+ 300	+ 310	− 10	0
Coffee	+ 14	+ 656	+ 18	+ 1
Tea	+ 204	+ 21	+ 2	+ 13
Cocoa beans	+ 100	+ 256	+ 15	+ 8
Total Foods	+12,291	+ 7,963	− 2,119	− 864
Oilseeds	+ 1,509	+ 5,279	− 37	− 18
Oilcake	+ 604	+ 1,312	− 140	− 199
Feed grains	+ 4,518	+ 6,482	− 1,730	− 407
Total Feeds	+ 6,631	+ 13,073	− 1,907	− 624
Total Foods and Feeds	+18,922	+ 21,036	− 4,026	−1,488

* Estonia, Latvia, Lithuania, Poland, Hungary, Yugoslavia, Rumania, Bulgaria, Albania

Source: M. K. Bennett, *Food for Postwar Europe*, Food Research Institute, Stanford University, March 1944

Herbert Hoover in his *Report on the World Famine* at Ottawa on June 28, 1946, emphasized that "France and North Africa will require 2.5 million tons less of food imports than during the past year."

Since the OFAR published its report in early July, other crop reports have arrived which seem to brighten the picture. Based on all available reports we estimate the *actual requirements of Continental Europe* at *"8.5–9 million tons of wheat, grains for food, and dry legumes."*

This estimate does not consider possible imports of wheat from Rumania and corn from Yugoslavia, which would increase the net imports.

The 8.5–9 million tons compare with prewar imports of wheat and rye (including inter-European) of 5–6 million tons and feed grain imports of approximately 6.4 million tons.

The need for feed grains will be less than in prewar times because of the much smaller livestock holdings, but larger than the imports that can be expected.

Europe's Self-Sufficiency in Food Was Growing Before the War

As shown in Table 4-1, Continental Europe before the war was an importer chiefly of wheat, feed grains and oilseeds, and an exporter of a variety of livestock products. Due to better farming methods and a steady increase in the use of fertilizer, the beginning of the war found it nearly self-supporting as to sugar and well on its way to self-sufficiency in wheat.

The total *net imports* of wheat in 1934-1938 *averaged 179* million bushels, or less than half of its requirements 10 years before. In addition, an average of 294 million bushels of corn were imported for the livestock.

Livestock production, except in the Danubian states, was therefore a secondary production insofar as it relied heavily on the imports of feed grains and of oilcake equivalent. Oilseeds, which on the average of the years 1934–38 were imported at an oil equivalent of approximately 4 million short tons, provided both the bulk of the fat requirements for the population of the industrialized countries, and high protein feed. So much of this feed was used that in addition to oilcake produced in the

European oil mills from imports of oilseed, approximately 1.3 million tons of oilcake were imported from the Far East outright. Europe, therefore, was far from self-sufficient before the war in the feed required for its livestock and livestock product exports.

Imports to the various European countries came in part from the Continent itself, mainly from the Danubian countries: Hungary, Rumania, Yugoslavia and Bulgaria—Europe's granary. These four countries exported on the average of the years 1934-38 approximately 70 million bushels of wheat and rye, and nearly the same amount of feed grains to Central and Western Europe. Imports from Russia varied heavily from year to year, averaging about 250,000 bushels of food grains and 160,000 bushels of feed grains a year. With increasing yields per acre, in many European countries the exports of food grains from the four overseas exporting countries were decreasing steadily since the Twenties.

A Fundamental Change:
From Grain to Root Feeding

During the thirties, when trade restrictions and lack of foreign currency weighed heavily on many countries, *a shift in livestock feeding from grain feeding to root feeding occurred.*

Roots such as potatoes, fodder, beets and sugar beet tops had always been used for feed in Germany because they are admirably suited to a country with limited acreage but cheap labor, their yield per acre being several times that of grains. More and more acreage was devoted to root feeds in Germany, Austria and the Scandinavian countries.

One of the reasons why Germany and the countries it occupied could maintain food consumption on a relatively high level was that Germany forced its satellites to use a greater part of their acreage for direct human food, and to devote more and more acreage to the cultivation of root crops, both for human consumption and for feed. The same was done, out of necessity, by Switzerland and Sweden. It is due to this shift in farm production that the total crops in Holland, Belgium and Switzerland will be larger this year than they were before the war.

60

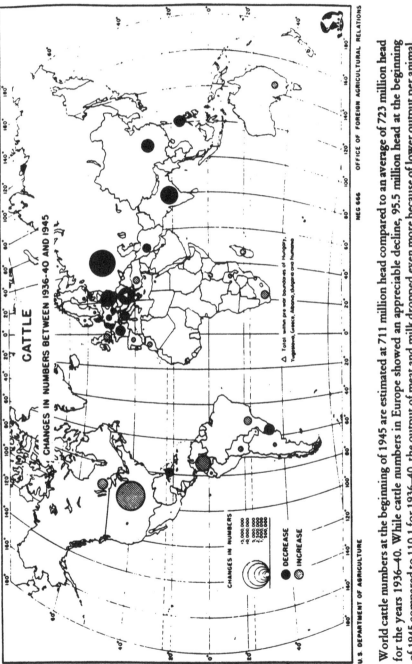

World cattle numbers at the beginning of 1945 are estimated at 711 million head compared to an average of 723 million head for the years 1936–40. While cattle numbers in Europe showed an appreciable decline, 95.5 million head at the beginning of 1945 compared to 110.1 for 1936–40, the output of meat and milk dropped even more because of lower output per animal.

Europe's Livestock Reduced During the War

Notwithstanding the higher yields from root crops, all European countries had to decrease their livestock during the war, retaining as much as possible of their cattle, but cutting down heavily on hogs and poultry. Heavy inroads into the livestock holdings occurred when actual warfare struck in nearly all European countries.

The Process of Rehabilitation

In the crop year 1946/47 Europe is more diversified as to the state of its agriculture than it ever was. Rehabilitation has taken a very different form in the various countries. In some countries the decrease of cattle does not amount to more than 6% or even less, while its decrease over the whole of Europe may be as high as 15%. The rate of the decrease of hogs was more uniform and amounted at the end of the war over the whole of Europe to 50–60%. Since then the number of hogs has been on the increase. The smaller livestock population means, of course, a drop in the need for feeds. Nevertheless *concentrated feeds are desperately needed nearly everywhere in Europe*. Oilcake and other high-protein feeds would not only allow for an increase in the cattle population, but *immediately increase the milk yield of the existing dairy cattle*. Also both because a rehabilitation of the livestock holdings are highly desired and because much acreage has been shifted from feed to direct food production, imports of feedgrains are urgently needed.

In Scandinavia, Switzerland, the Western European countries including Spain and Portugal, and also in Rumania and Bulgaria, the *acreage which has been cultivated in 1945/46 is about normal*. Except in Scandinavia, there was a lack of fertilizer and a shortage of agricultural equipment and of labor, but due to favorable weather the crops will be normal, or not far from normal. There will be more potatoes and less wheat. The output of livestock will be smaller in all of these countries, and in addition there will be *a gap in the fat and oil consumption* due to the lack of vegetable oil or oilseed imports from the Far East.

In some other countries, rehabilitation has made great strides, but the crops will not yet come up to normal. This applies to Italy, whose crops turned out much better than was expected; to

Yugoslavia, Czechoslovakia and Greece. Even Hungary is doing much better than last year and has cultivated most of its soil, though the total lack of equipment and loss of 80% of its cattle and hogs (according to a Swiss report) makes for a slow recovery.

The Real Trouble Spots: Germany and Austria

The real trouble spots are Germany, Austria and to a much greater degree Poland. This latter country not only suffered heavily from repeated warfare, but political strife and lack of adaptability of the peasant population are a decided handicap to any kind of reconstruction.

Germany, with an expected population of 65–70 million, one-sixth the population of Europe, *has lost 24% of its farm land*, but increased its population. It has been divided into four zones of occupation, of which the Russian zone has a relatively large share of the farm and potato land. While this zone will be self-supporting, *the 45 million Germans in the three other zones cannot live from the soil which is left*, and consequently will have to be fed. Austria, which has a population of only 7 million people, and is divided into four occupation zones, is not in the same predicament, but the Russian occupation army is living partly off the land. It is Germany and Austria which are upsetting Europe's food balance, as well as our own; or rather it is the fact that Germany has been divided into four zones, one of which lies behind the Iron Curtain, while Poland, which received part of Germany's crop land, is not yet able to produce an adequate crop.

The other trouble spot is the *lack of oilseed imports*, which means less meat, less fat, less milk and fewer eggs for every European consumer. This gap cannot be closed before imports from the Far East are again available. It has at present to be made good by an increase in the import of food grains.

The fact that sugar production will be 1/3 below prewar levels does not weigh heavily in the balance of food needs.

Food Grain Requirements of Continental Europe Before and After World War II

Countries	Population in millions[4]	Average import of wheat & flour 1936–38 in million metric tons	Hoover Allocation[1] May–Sept. 1946	Our Estimate for 1946/47 in mill. metric tons
France	39.1	0.80	1.75	0.50[2]
Holland	9.0	0.60	0.08	0.40
Belgium–Luxembourg	8.0	1.30	0.30	0.90
Switzerland	–	0.43	0.09	0.35
Spain	26.0	0.06	0.24	0.10
Portugal	8.0	0.05	0.02	0.10
Italy	41.5	0.80	0.78	0.90
Greece	7.5	0.60	0.28	0.70
Denmark	3.9	0.05	–	0.10
Sweden	6.2	0.05	–	–
Norway	3.0	0.20	0.01	0.30[3]
Finland	13.5	0.15	0.11	0.20
Czechoslovakia	–	0.15	0.29	0.05
Poland	24.5	–	0.34	0.30
Yugoslavia	16.0	–	0.25	–
Albania	1.0	–	0.02	–
Germany	65–68	0.84	–	–
American zone	18.0	–	–	–
British zone	23.3	–	1.37	3.00
French zone	6.0	–	–	–
Russian zone	23.3–25.3	–	–	–
Austria	7.0	0.25	0.23	0.50
Total		6.33	6.16	8.40

[1] The allocations of the Hoover Committee were for the five last most difficult months of the year 1945/46. Wealthy countries like Belgium and Switzerland bought in advance. With the poor countries the whole deficit appeared in May–September 1946.

[2] Considering the declaration of Hoover that France and French North Africa would require 2.5 million tons of wheat less in this new crop year.

[3] Claimed at the FAO meeting in May 400,000 tons, but crops improved.

[4] Population figures used in this table are those used by the Hoover Committee for its food allocations.

Germany Cannot be "Pastorized"

In 1937 Germany produced about 85% of its total food. In the war year 1943/44 it imported about 7 million tons of food for the needs of a population of about 68 million. Today the population figure may reach 65 to 68 million, but the crop land is only 76% of the former area. The American commander in Germany described the situation as follows to the Hoover Committee:[3]

"It has lost 24% of its agricultural area—an area capable of producing surplus food form some 4 million people.

"It is hardly possible to make Germany a predominantly agricultural country—the remaining 21 million hectares of land in farms would have to support three persons per hectare. On an acreage basis that is only three-fourths of an acre per person compared to over 7 acres per person in the United States. About 80% of the people in the past years were engaged in occupations other than agriculture.

"Interzonal movement of food and trade in Germany is necessary to make maximum use of the resources. In general this was a movement of industrial products to the East and of food products, especially grain, to the West.

"The U.S. Zone is now and has always been a food deficit area, requiring in 1943/44 imports of some 2 million tons of food.

"The stoppage of interzonal food shipments and foreign trade leaves no alternative to relief shipments until the German economy has been reestablished on a workable basis.

"The crop now growing has been planted largely without fertilizer and a minimum amount of farm supplies and equipment necessary to maximize production. Without a weather miracle the coming harvest will be lower and the food situation in the U.S. Zone even more serious than in the year just passed.

"General McNarney emphasized that the statistics would indicate the problem from a nutritional viewpoint and also from a humanitarian viewpoint. However, the need for food in Germany should not be considered merely from a humanitarian viewpoint, as food is essential not only to the economic recovery of Germany, but also to the recovery of Europe as a whole.

"Germany's inventory has been exhausted, and the essential commodities of life are no longer available. Economic recovery is almost at a standstill.

"German transport facilities are required to move relief supplies and exports across Europe. German workmen must be used to man available German transport facilities. German coal is vital to Europe. German potash, salt, lumber, spare parts and other products are needed throughout Europe.

"Coal production in the Ruhr has decreased substantially since the recent food cut. Production cannot be increased until there is a requisite supporting economy. The pump can be primed only with food. Without food Germany cannot produce coal. Without coal it cannot support minimum transportation and industry. Without coal Germany cannot produce fertilizer, and unless it produces fertilizer it is unable to improve its own food supply.

"The inability of the German economy to recover increases the cost of occupation. It makes fewer supplies available in Germany to support the occupation forces. It lengthens the period in which essential imports must be financed by the United States.

"A long continuation of low food rations, with the economy at a standstill as a result, may lead to unrest which will necessitate a larger army of occupation than is now contemplated, for a longer period of time.

"The political effects of an inadequate food ration may be felt in central Europe for years. American policy requires every effort to be made to democratize Germany and to create an atmosphere of political freedom. Political stability in Germany is closely related to political freedom. Political stability cannot develop under conditions which create political apathy. Political apathy cannot be overcome in a population which must devote its full effort to a daily search for food."

How Many Imports Will be Needed for 1946/47?

The Russian Zone

The division of Germany into four zones has the disagreeable consequence that only the Russian zone, embracing about one-fourth of the remaining German territory—which together with the provinces lost to Poland used to be Germany's grain and potato larder—seems to be near self-sustenance. It evidently also supports the Russian occupation army.

The official rations are reported to be about 1400 calories a day in the cities, while the rural population is evidently faring better.

Within the zone a redistribution and dividing up of large estates seems to have taken place, which as a rule means a decrease of agricultural production for some years.

The Russians, nevertheless, emphasize that the rations in their zone are higher than those of the three other zones.

The Non-Russian Zones

From the *U.S. zone*, a predominantly agricultural zone comprising a population of about 18 million people, it was reported that in April there were "only supplies on hand and on the water" to assure 915 calories a day per person until September.

The actual ration was down in April to 1275 calories at the most, still further down to 1180 in May, but from then on it turned upwards. To bring the ration up to the goal of 1550 calories, the import of about 82,500 tons per month is needed until the end of September.

The *British zone*, with 20 million people, including the industrial centers of the Ruhr and the Rhineland, labored under even more difficult conditions. Already in early spring the official ration was gradually reduced to 1000 calories a day. This was the only zone where food riots occurred. The cutting of the miners' rations in the Ruhr caused great damage, because the production of coal was thereby reduced for months. The British Food Minister explained on July 4th that only to maintain the 1000 calories daily for this area he needed 130,000 metric tons of wheat or wheat equivalent per month, and he urged the United States to send them.

The *French zone*, with 6 million people, predominantly agricultural, had to feed the occupation army; nevertheless, our general impression is that the food situation in this area (Baden-Württemberg, etc.) was approximately the same as in the American zone.

Berlin lived under conditions which were certainly no better than in the American zone, but not as bad as in the British. Small garden plots (similar to our wartime "victory gardens"), which are popular there, seem to help the population at the present time.

The Hoover Committee put the requirement of imports for the non-Russian zones from May to September at 1.37 million tons of wheat or wheat equivalent (British zone 900,000 tons, American zone 275,000 tons, French zone 195,000 tons).

If these ratios were applied to the whole year, they would mean an allocation of 261,400 tons per month, i.e., 3.1 million tons per year.

We assume that not much less than 3 million tons of grain will be imported into Germany by the end of the 1947 harvest. The actual import requirements will be much less during the first six months after the crops have been harvested, but will increase again next spring.

The total crop output has been estimated at 70% of prewar in the Russian zone, and at perhaps 90% in the others.

The loss of livestock is estimated at 20% for cows, and 60% for hogs; the greatest losses are in the Soviet and French zones, while in the American zone cattle losses are only 5% and hogs 50%. Of the horses in the Soviet zone, about two-thirds have disappeared. In the other zones the loss of horses was not as great as that.

While the decrease of all livestock frees land for the cultivation of food grains, which was formerly used for feed, the loss of horses is a great handicap for all agricultural production. The tractor is as good as unknown on small and medium-sized farms in Germany. There is no doubt that the German agriculture will make great efforts to produce greater quantities in 1946/47 than in 1945/46. Almost all progress, however, will depend on the help which the allied nations will give the Germans. If Germany would have to remain within the rations of 1550 calories, imports in 1946/47 could be lower than 3.1 million tons. If, however, the aim shall be to put Germany, whose climate claims a larger food consumption than in the warmer countries, into a position to work again, and to pay for the inevitable imports of raw materials, foods and feeds, then the country cannot stay within those low rations. Our estimate of 3 million tons of food imports should be the maximum.

Germany's Food Economy in the Future

It was not difficult to predict that the Potsdam Agreement would put a burden on us of $300-400 million a year to be spent for food, feed and other imports. This was our estimate on September 3, 1946 (see *Barron's Weekly*). We called these amounts "inverse reparations".

A comprehensive plan, drafted by the Allied Control Council in Berlin, partly published in April 1946[4], and partly not yet published, tries to outline an economic setup for Germany which might enable the country to produce so much food in 1949/50 that the Germans can consume as much as they did in the depression year of 1935. The following assumptions were made:

The German industries, insofar as absolutely needed for food production and other vital civilian necessities, will not be dismantled for some years, even if they are usable for war purposes (like chemical fertilizer factories).

An overall land-utilization plan has been drafted (but not published) providing for a reduction of forests and trying to maximize the crop yield per acre.

Exports from Germany are scheduled to reach 3 billion marks ($1.2 billion in 1936 values). This would be as much as 71% of the German exports in that year.

Of these amounts the Germans will be allowed to spend 1.5 billion marks ($600 million) "to pay for any imports of food and fodder required". This assumes that the livestock holdings will be rebuilt and that the total imports of food and feed will amount to 6.5 million tons of wheat or wheat equivalent. That is practically identical with our estimate, as published on September 3, 1945, that when Germany's livestock herds would be rebuilt, 6–7 million tons of grains, of which 4 million tons would be for feed purposes, would have to be imported.

We cannot agree with the plan in all points. The feed requirements—if livestock should be rebuilt to the level of 1932—will probably be correct. We have the greatest doubts, however, whether the surplus of German exports after paying for the imports of raw materials will allow for such high feed imports after four to five years. For the first years the need for raw material imports into Germany is certainly underestimated, while the speed with which the country will adapt itself to the loss of 24% of its acreage is overestimated. We think that it is still safe to stick to our conclusions that:

1. The United States will have to support Germany with food to the extent of at least $300-400 million a year for a number of years;

2. In time, Germany will build up self-sufficiency through agricultural development and through an "ersatz" economy;

3. As a final result, its potential for war may be partly re-created.[5]

Austria

When the small republic of Austria emerged from the 1919 peace conference in Versailles as a country of 6 million inhabitants, of which one-third lived in the capital, Vienna, not many believed that this fragile fragment of the old Austrian empire would ever become self-sustaining. For more than a decade, loans from the Allies were needed almost every year.

Austria's urban population starved bitterly for several years after World War I. Then the quasi-miracle happened: Austria, by applying modern agricultural techniques, and especially chemical fertilizers, reached a relatively high degree of self-sufficiency. On the mostly mountainous soil it produced 70% of its food grains, 75% of its fats and oils, and 100% of its sugar. Grain imports in the Thirties were about 100,000 tons a year. Austria earned so much as a trading, banking and transportation center that from about 1934 on it was economically self-sufficient. When Hitler seized his own fatherland, Austria, "in order to provide Lebensraum" for that country, the Austrians were actually already standing on their own feet with sufficient "Lebensraum".

The second World War became a greater catastrophe for the country than the first because this time it became a theater of war. Like Germany, it was divided into four zones of occupation, and the Russians and French are living "off the land".

General Mark Clark told the Hoover Committee that the harvest of 1945 was less than half of normal. As in Germany, the Allies tried to maintain a 1550-calorie daily diet, but failed to do so from spring 1946 on. From that time on, the Soviet zone received only allocations of 800–1200 calories, while the allocations in Vienna fluctuated between 1100 and 1400 calories.

The United Nations Relief and Rehabilitation Administration (UNRRA) tried to step in. Until the end of May it has imported 280,000 metric tons of commodities, of which only 86,000 metric tons were food. The Hoover Committee was requested by the American commanding officer to see to it that from May to September 300,000 tons of cereals be allocated to maintain a 1200-calorie diet in the cities. Evidently impressed by figures of a high death rate in Vienna, the committee agreed to propose the shipment of 225,000 tons.

It is now reported that the American zone in Austria will produce 90% of the food of a normal prewar year. In the other zones progress is said to be much slower, bringing the total to perhaps 65-70% of normal.

The volume to be imported in 1946/47 into Austria, which may now have close to 7 million inhabitants, may be assumed to be higher than the 225,000 tons appropriated by Hoover in 1946.

Future prospects look relatively favorable, mainly due to the fact that Austria found oil under its soil during the war.

France

Before the war, with the aid of its North African possessions, France, now a country of about 38.5 million people, was nearly self-sufficient in cereals and grains, except for corn. There were moderate imports of sugar as well as large imports of oilseeds and vegetable oil from France's mandates and colonies in Central Africa. Under German occupation, France sharply increased its potato and other root crop production.

The drought in North Africa and bad weather in France, together with the unsettled conditions of the last war year, necessitated large food imports in the spring and summer of this year. Some 343 million bushels of wheat, considerably more than France ever imported, will be shipped into the country between May and September. Matters were made more difficult by the fact that farmers are evidently holding back deliveries (as stated by

Swiss reports on the basis of critical memos made by French trade associations). Vegetable oils from its own colonies, normally amounting to 300,000 tons, could not be brought in sufficient quantities, though available, because the Combined Food Board did not allocate more than 144,000 tons to France.[6] Discussions about an increase of the allocations are still going on.

All statistics on production should be closely scrutinized, as the official figures certainly are understatements. It seems that even in the spring of 1946 the farm population had been living well; unfortunately the distribution is very unequal.

As of June 15th, all crops were reported to be highly satisfactory. A normal acreage had been planted, the weather was excellent and the supply of fertilizer was reported to be adequate. The wheat crop, normally amounting to 8.8 million tons, will be between 7-8.5 million tons, which is much higher than last year. Sugar under the incentive of higher prices has increased to 85% of normal production and the potato crop is much greater than prewar; also the grape crop, so important because the French are used to getting a considerable part of their calorie intake from wine, is said to be good, and rations have been doubled in July. With its cattle holding at about 95% of normal, France should be doing well, if adequate imports of oilseeds become possible.

French North Africa also will have a good harvest of grains and oil, though not quite up to normal. Probably it will not yet be able to take up its customary exports of wheat, and small imports of this grain from the outside into France may therefore become necessary. We can accept the figure of Herbert Hoover that France and its North African possessions alone will need 94.0 million bushels less than last year.

Belgium

Belgium, with 8.4 million people, is a highly industrialized country with a large urban population and a scarcity of agricultural land. Before the war it was dependent on food imports up to 50%. Farms are small and are used to a large degree for livestock production. In spite of its population of only 8.4 million Belgium was Europe's second largest wheat importer, and one of its main importers of corn and vegetable oil. During the war Germany enforced a shift to greater production of direct human food, such as wheat, potatoes and rapeseed. Consequently the output of livestock products declined sharply, though the number of cattle remained at nearly prewar heights.

At the FAO meeting in May 1946, the Belgian representative reported that his country had lent 100,000 tons of wheat to France, which it did not get back on time, and therefore was down to an official rate of 1585 calories per day. Nevertheless the country did not belong to those which really were badly off, nor did it pretend to be.

During the last year the number of hogs has increased by 40%, and all livestock holdings will soon be back at prewar levels. Direct reports from Belgium show convincingly that the food situation in the last months was considerably better than in other countries. Much food seemed to be finding its way into the black markets in France. The outlook for the new harvest is very good. Livestock output will be back to normal as soon as enough feed is available. Since Belgium is getting imports from Argentina, it might soon receive sufficient amounts of corn and sunflower seeds for this purpose. At present it is reported as trying to buy wheat from Turkey.

Belgium has always relied on foreign imports, and will continue to do so. Heavy exports of industrial goods, which are already taking place, make this possible. There is no reason why we should wish that it were to become more self-sufficient than it used to be. We may soon welcome export possibilities like these.

Holland

Holland has done an amazing job of rehabilitation. Visitors report that conditions are quickly improving. Food supplies are satisfactory, though meat and fats are still scarce. Fish, vegetables and potatoes are freely available. Bread is rationed, but at liberal amounts.

The acreage is fully cultivated, and where the sea overflowed the land, grass has already been sown and cattle are grazing. Crop returns are greater than in prewar times, since much of the pasture has been turned over to grain cultivation. Wheat production, though considerably higher than last year, will not yet be up to normal, but a much greater than prewar potato crop will make up for the difference. Sugar production, likewise higher than last year, will be only 50–60% of prewar times. For several months Holland has been producing a large surplus of vegetables which it is unable to export. Its two prewar customers for this commodity were Germany and Great Britain, and while Germany is unable to import, Great Britain evidently does not care to spend its foreign exchange on vegetables.

Holland has always been famous as an exporter of livestock products; it exceeded all other countries in the export of processed milk. Excellent pasture and heavy imports of oilseeds from its Far Eastern colonies made this intensive livestock production possible. At present the number of cattle is about 20% lower than in prewar times, though it has already increased since last year. Milk yields per cow are lower than normal, due to the lack of concentrate feed during the winter, and the fact that not enough fertilizer is available for the pastures. Thus total milk production is at present only 70% of prewar. While milk and butter are still rationed, small exports of cheese were to start in June. Holland is also ready to export condensed milk, but is having difficulty in getting the coal which is needed for the milk condensing plants.

Like Denmark, it is eager to regain its prewar customers and does not hesitate to ration its citizens in order to do so. Exports of livestock products on a large scale, however, will not be possible before more feed is at hand. Imports of feed grains would do much to rebuild the hog herds and poultry flocks, but for the dairy herds oilcake is needed additionally. Feed imports and sufficient amounts of fertilizer would very quickly bring the Dutch food production and food exports back to normal. No higher wheat imports than prior to the war will probably be needed in 1946/47, rather considerably less.

Switzerland

Switzerland with its 4 million people is at present one of the richest small countries in the world. While its wealth is due primarily to its highly specialized manufacturing industries, it has always been famous for its dairy industry. The country with its mountain regions is not too well suited for grain cultivation, but the first World War had so strongly impressed the importance of food self-sufficiency on the habitants that as much as possible was done to increase domestic grain production. The livestock industries were, at the beginning of World War II, only to a minor part dependent on imported feed. The importance of livestock production within the agricultural sector can be measured from the fact that the receipts from livestock products amount to 75-80% of all the receipts from agriculture. Swiss farms are small and there is very little absentee ownership.

Hogs, whose number was always small, are as in Denmark a by-product of the dairy industries and, where possible, are fed potatoes in addition to skim milk. Something like a diplomatic incident occurred when some weeks ago an American reporter, after having seen so many war-devastated countries, visited Switzerland. He took a look at some farms and reported with disgust that in Switzerland the hogs were being fed better than human beings in the countries he had just left, since these animals were fed meat and potatoes. He could not have been expected to know, of course, that potato feeding is much more economical than our grain feeding, but the ire in Switzerland was great.

Switzerland has weathered the war well. As it had to, the indigenous production rose, through a shift from pasture and feed grains to more grains for human consumption and to potatoes. Until 1944 imports, especially from Argentina, were possible, but at the end of 1944 and in the first half of 1945 the food situation was tight, with potatoes the mainstay of the diet.

While the number of horses working as draft power, because of the lack of gasoline, had increased, the number of all other animals had decreased during the war, most of all that of chickens. Since then some rebuilding of herds has taken place. At present, there are 15% fewer cattle and 25% fewer hogs than in 1939, but chickens have increased again to 95% of prewar. Switzerland had always been an importer of eggs, and the lack of eggs had been very keenly felt. There was great rejoicing when following the visit here of the most interesting personality in the Swiss food business, the first eggs from the United States arrived just in time for Easter, and eggs could be decorated and derationed.

Food consumption is well on its way to normal levels in spite of rationing of meat, fats and bread. Swiss businessmen doubt whether bread rationing is actually needed or whether it is meant to show off that Switzerland is "ready for any sacrifice".

The harvest promises to become good. Switzerland, which increased its self-sufficiency during the war, will have to import less wheat and feed grains than in normal times.

Spain

Spain suffered so heavily from its civil war that agricultural production never returned to normal. In addition there was a very severe drought last year. Relatively large imports were therefore needed.

Before its civil war, Spain was self-sufficient as to wheat, most other grains and livestock products. It was the chief exporter of olive oil and made very considerable exports of oranges, rice and potatoes.

This harvest will be the first really good one that Spain had since the middle Thirties. The grain, olive, orange and grape crops are in excellent condition, and so are potatoes and legumes. The wheat crop is expected to be 141 million bushels, which compares favorably with an average of 143 million bushels in 1926-30 and 160 million bushels in 1931-35. Daily bread rations have already been revised by 100 grams as of the middle of July, and rumors were even spreading that the government was selling wheat to UNRRA. Imports of food will be small. Soybean oil from the United States will be exchanged for olive oil, and it seems that the first shipments are on their way.

Portugal, *which was likewise hit by the drought last year, is having good crops this year.*

Italy

Italy suffered heavily in 1945 from actual warfare, economic disturbances of all kinds and from the drought. The food situation was very bad during the early months of 1946. Italy received 4.5 bushels of wheat up to March 1st and allocations of the Hoover Committee amounted to 28.5 million bushels for the months May to September. With shipments of wheat arriving in the ports and good crops being harvested, the government has already been able to raise the daily bread ration to 250 grams and to increase the highly important spaghetti ration. Milk has just been derationed.

Under Mussolini Italy had moved closer to self-sufficiency, but imports of approximately 20 million tons of olive oil and of vegetable oil were still necessary.

This spring the acreage was fully cultivated, though there was a shortage of seed, fertilizer and draftpower. The wheat crop is expected to be at least 40% higher than last year, though still somewhat under normal. The olive oil crop is likewise expected to be good and so is the sugar crop, both of which were very poor last year. Italy's import needs will thus be much smaller than last year's.

Nevertheless the indigenous food production will not be sufficient, for it never was, and since exports will not be large enough to allow for liberal imports, the food situation will remain tight for the poorer part of the urban population. The black market is highly developed and distribution is badly organized.

UNRRA is doing an excellent job of rehabilitation, especially in the agricultural sector. It is to be hoped that this part of its work will be continued.

Greece

Greece with its 7 million people was always far from self-sufficient. It exported currants and raisins on a large scale, as well as tobacco and olives, and imported approximately 30% of the wheat it needed in addition to rice.

Greece has suffered heavily from the war. Last year's drought aggravated its sufferings. Draft animals and agricultural equipment are lacking, the distribution of the available food is badly organized, and political strife is hampering rehabilitation.

Weather conditions this year, however, have been excellent, and crops will be much improved over last year. The wheat crop is estimated at 25-26.5 million bushels, which compares with 22 million on the average of the years 1931-35, and 36 million bushels in 1938. Generally crops are estimated at 85% of normal, which would be an increase of 20% over last year's. Wheat imports, however, might be larger than in prewar times, when they fluctuated around 17 million bushels. Rehabilitation work like that of the UNRRA will still be needed.

Denmark

Denmark, although a small country with less than 4 million inhabitants, was, until the war, *the world's main exporter of butter, bacon and eggs.* Of the 857 million pounds of total world exports of bacon, Denmark furnished 419 million pounds, or nearly 50%,, and in addition 25% of the total world export of butter and of eggs. Its main competitors were Canada, Australia and New Zealand.

Scientific Cooperative Farming

Livestock raising on small farms has been the chief industry of the country and its main source of foreign exchange. Danish farming is unique. It is thoroughly commercialized and specialized. For decades Danish agriculture has made use of everything that the highest grade of scientific research can provide. *Though farming is done on a completely individualistic basis, it is nevertheless governed by centralized planning.* But neither the government nor any other officialdom has anything to do with this planning. The authority which rules agriculture is the voluntary cooperation of the farmers. Planning is needed, because the farming is geared to exports, and the export markets have become ever more uncertain since the end of the Twenties.

All farmers belong to at least one cooperative, and many to several. The cooperatives in turn are working together and have formed a joint council, which in many respects takes the place of our Department of Agriculture. Before the war, 86.2% of all the butter was produced in cooperative creameries, and 75% of all hogs which came to market were slaughtered in cooperative packing plants, which also did the wholesaling and part of the export business.

Most of the farming is done by the farmer and his family. Electricity is widely used, but tractors are practically non-existent, except on some of the very large farms.

The Danish cows had the world's highest yield of butterfat before the war. Feed of all kinds was one of the few items whose import was not restricted before the war. Feed grains, oilseeds and oilcake were imported from all over the world. A shift had occurred from the indigenous production of feed grains to roots, such as fodder beets and potatoes. Hogs were a by-product of dairy farming and were in addition fed boiled potatoes.

Denmark was very lucky because *it escaped actual warfare.* The Germans, under the occupation, exploited the country by exporting food and importing raw materials on a much smaller scale, but they destroyed nothing. The valuable cattle holdings were, when the Germans left, only 8% less than in 1939. The hog and poultry herds, which increased somewhat since last year, are now between 55 and 60% of prewar. Without substantial imports of feed they cannot be increased further. The country, during the war, produced enough grain for human consumption, but would like to shift back to producing more feed. Feed grains as well as oilseeds are urgently needed to increase exports of livestock products.

The Danish population was one of the best fed in Europe during the whole war. There is rationing of meat, butter and bread, but the rations are liberal—to say the least.

Food Exports Never Stopped

Denmark has never stopped exporting food. When the war was over it shifted the direction of its exports away from Germany to England. The United Kingdom had always been Denmark's main customer, while Germany occupied second place and was not to be counted on too much. There were practically no other customers, and the United Kingdom, therefore, had a monopsony and was in a position to set the price. At present, it would like to buy Denmark's total livestock production, but the prices it is offering are so low that—as the Danes explain—they do not cover the farmers' costs, and farming for export would have to be subsidized by the government.

On the other hand, there are other buyers, notably Russia, who want to purchase the total output as far as it is not allocated by the Combined Food Board, or the IEFC to Great Britain or other countries. Russia is not only offering much better prices, but wants to pay in oilseeds and sunflower seeds, which Denmark used to import from Russia, and which would enable it to increase its dairy production instantly, as well as to produce and export oleomargarine. The choice is a difficult one, because none of the Scandinavian countries want to rely too heavily on Russia, and Denmark will need the English market as soon as the emergency is over.

Denmark has to be regarded as a food exporter. It will import feed grains if it can get them, but is already exporting butter, meat, eggs, beef, cattle, horses and some sugar. Denmark is one of those countries which is worried about the fact that the Americas have increased their livestock production and exports.

Sweden

The Swedes, now a nation of not quite 6.5 million people in a country one-sixth larger than California, have emerged from the war stronger than ever.

Some 60% of Sweden is still covered by forests, of which the country is making excellent use.

Swedish Agriculture Makes the Country Almost Self-Sufficient

Only in the south of the country does Sweden's agriculture work under favorable conditions. Flowers do not bloom in Stockholm before mid-summertime. Further north conditions are even less suitable for farming. Farmers' cooperatives have not yet reached the perfection of the Danish or the Finnish ones. Nevertheless, Sweden has become *as good as self-sufficient for all important foodstuffs, except fats, and is even exporting livestock products on the basis of imported feed.*

Two generations ago, it would have been almost unthinkable to grow wheat on a large scale in regions as far north as Sweden. By better selection of seeds and plant breeding, however, Sweden has managed to produce larger and larger parts of its wheat consumption on its own soil. The government assisted this effort by enforcing an admixture of Swedish home-grown wheat so that an increasing part of all wheat consumed had to be Swedish.

Fish, which is abundant, is a valuable addition to the daily diet.

Sweden had strict rationing during the war, but consumption was at relatively high levels. During most of the time the country was able to import some corn and oilseeds from South America. The cattle population, therefore, is nearly as high as it was before the war, while egg production is only slightly under normal and the number of hogs is only 15% lower than in prewar times.

All during the war, Sweden had been helping its neighbors, Norway and Finland. Immediately after the war was over, credits were granted to these two countries, and food of all kinds exported. Community kitchens were set up and provided with food from Sweden in both countries.

Sweden is self-sufficient as to wheat, and if the harvest is fair to good it will not need imports of wheat. Corn and oilseeds will probably be imported from Argentina. Sweden is in the fortunate position to be able to offer industrial goods in exchange for feeds. It can be expected that it will continue to export livestock products, especially to Norway and Finland.

Norway

Norway is a country of about 125,000 square miles, about the size of Mexico, reaching from the North where the sun does not rise for months in the winter, to the temperate regions of Oslo. So little of the soil can be used for farming that only 2.8% of the whole area is under cultivation. Nearly one-fourth of the country is still covered with forests, but by far the larger part of Norway's area, including its 150,000 islands, is barren and not used in any way.

The approximately 3 million people would be very poor were it not for Norway's three great assets: the sea, which makes possible the fishing industry, whaling and the income of the merchant marine; the *cheap water power,* and the *forests.*

Norway, with a population of 3 million produced enough milk, butter and cheese to be a net exporter, though on a very small scale, but imported some meat and 90% of the grain for human consumption, feed grains, oilseeds and fruit. Its hog holdings were small as compared with Denmark and Sweden, but there were in addition sheep in those parts of the country where the pasture was not sufficiently good for cows. Fish, of course, is eaten widely and cod liver oil is a must in a country where there is so little sun most of the year.

During the war Norway gained somewhat in self-sufficiency, taking approximately 10% more acreage under cultivation and producing one-third more potatoes. The output of grains last year was greater than during the war, but Norway will always have to rely on wheat imports. The cattle herds are only 5% lower than in prewar times, but the yield per cow has decreased because not enough oilseeds can be imported. The fish catches are excellent and fish in 1945/46 was the mainstay of the diet. The fat Norwegian herring is used to provide part of the demand for oil. More fish could be exported if the demand were larger.

Whaling was resumed last winter, but the output was only one-third of normal, since parts of the whaling fleet were destroyed. The new season begins in early winter and promises to become better.

The new harvest is likely to become good. Ample fertilizer was available, since Norway has large nitrogen factories.

Norway will not need larger imports than in prewar times, except for daily products and meat. There is no reason to wish that it should be self-sufficient, since it can pay for its imports with the receipts of whaling, fishing, the merchant fleet and the output of its forests.

Poland

At the war's end this nation was reduced from a population of 35 million to 24 million. Poland lost its provinces east of the Curzon Line, populated mostly by White Russians, but gained a good deal of Germany's best food provinces, including valuable industries, communication lines and ports.

The mainstay of Poland's prewar agriculture was grain and potatoes, of which it was an exporter. It also exported bacon and pork, but it did not have a commercialized, scientifically managed livestock industry as the Western and Northern European countries did. On the contrary, farming generally was on a very primitive level. Very few machines were used. A large percentage of the farm land was in the hands of the Polish aristocracy and of the Catholic Church, and both did little to improve agricultural techniques.

Poland has suffered more from the war than nearly any other country. Actual warfare raged several times. The country is devastated; a very large part of the livestock—40% of the cattle—is lost. The large estates, except those belonging to the Church, are being divided up, and political unrest is making the reorganization even more difficult. Instead of exporting agricultural surplus, the country was not able to provide for the urban population, and in spite of vigorous help from UNRRA, the caloric rate for the non-self-supporting population was only 1300 calories in May 1946, and was still dropping.

In addition to sending food, UNRRA is trying to rebuild the productive capacity of the country. Hatching eggs have been sent by plane from the United States, young chickens and horses from Denmark; Polish soldiers are trained in servicing tractors which UNRRA imported from Canada. Seeds of all kinds have been provided. Nevertheless, the representative from Poland to the FAO requested an additional import of almost 700,000 tons of wheat for 1946/47, of which 350,000 should be should be seeds; it seems that he did not convince the CFB that his country's own effort was adequate.

While it will take time until Poland has been rebuilt, the agricultural sector will be the first to return to tolerable conditions, in spite of the very gloomy official forecasts. The OFAR, which normally avoids any criticism of utterances by foreign governments, emphasized in its report of July 29th that reports from Poland indicate the official forecasts of acreage and yields are unduly pessimistic.

Even so, the outlook remains far from good. Since, however, the drought which prevailed has been broken, it can be assumed that Poland will be able to support its own population with the help of only small amounts of grain imports. Exports cannot yet be expected. Poland will still need help to rehabilitate its agriculture, such as seeds, fertilizer, draft power and livestock. But as soon as the grain has been threshed, which will be some time at the end of October or in November, it will be about able to take care of its urban population.

Czechoslovakia

Czechoslovakia, with a population of 14.7 million before the war, suffered some war devastation, but its resources were relatively well preserved. Its crop in 1945/46 was considerably smaller than normal, livestock holdings had declined by 25%, and the Russian army had lived off the land for a short time. The country, therefore, needed imports of about one-half million long tons of food, and some other help from UNRRA, but the majority of the population was living better than in most other European countries. There was some hoarding by the farmers, and the government had to announce special premiums to collect additional grain. Exports of sugar, malt and hops were made, though on a small scale. The last reports showed an improvement in the food situation, and a decrease in the importance of the black market.

Czechoslovakia was a rich agricultural country and will be so again within a short time. It exported wheat, barley and malt, and was one of the main European sugar exporters, while it imported feed grains and fats, mainly from the Danubian countries. Through the war it has lost 2.5–3% of its population, namely the

Sudeten-Germans whom it wanted to get rid of, but whom it will take time to replace. For this reason Czechoslovakia will be one of the few European countries where the soil will not be fully cultivated in 1946/47.

Nevertheless, Czechoslovakia will be quite capable of feeding herself, and even exporting. Some shift from less barley to more wheat production has been announced, but this will only be temporary. Czechoslovakia had something like a monopoly in brewery wheat, and it will try everything in its power to re-establish it as soon as the IEFC will allow it to export malt to overseas countries.

The outlook for the new crop is bright. Czechoslovakia will export more sugar, barley and malt than in the 1945/46 crop year. It will increase its livestock holdings if it can import feed grains from Rumania, or in exchange for industrial products. Trade agreements with Switzerland and Scandinavian countries, covering agricultural exports, were negotiated some time ago.

U.S.S.R.

Some 190 million Russians, living on one-sixth of the surface of the world, are at present anxiously watching their crops. A good harvest is highly desired after so many difficult years. The crop reports that emanate from Russia do not give a clear picture. However, it seems that the Ukraine will have a harvest below normal, but that most other regions, mainly in the south and Siberia, will fare better. While reports from Russia forecast the abolition of bread rationing soon after the harvest, OFAR in its report of July 29th is much more gloomy. The overall grain yield per acre is reported not likely to exceed the low average of recent years, and may be below that average. However, the acreage under cultivation is decidedly larger than last year, though not yet up to normal, *and the total output of grains will therefore exceed that of last year.* Rapid ripening of winter grain is facilitating the transition from the old to the new crop year.

Russia is eager to rebuild its livestock holdings, which have been badly reduced by the Germans. It seems, however, that this year's feed crop does not favor such intentions. On the other hand, Russia has offered oilseeds, which yield the more valuable feed and oilcake, to Denmark in exchange for livestock products.

Russia did not join UNRRA, nor did it cooperate with the Hoover Committee or any other relief work. It sent some wheat to France before the French election, but that can be discounted as a political move, as can some small help to Albania.

UNRRA helped the Ukraine until the end of May 1946, by sending 200,000 metric tons of goods, more than one-third of its food. Byelorussia received 84,000 tons of goods, 69,000 tons of which was food.

We are mainly interested in the question *whether the USSR will allow the countries* behind the Iron Curtain, which it dominates, *to export their surplus to Central and Western Europe.* It has a claim on Rumanian grains on reparation account,[7] and has been drawing on the Hungarian resources until recently. It seems to us that Russia will want machinery more than grains, especially for its political satellites. We therefore believe that it will encourage Rumania, Yugoslavia and Bulgaria to export their surplus of farm products against machinery and all kinds of equipment. Some discussions going on in Switzerland and elsewhere point in that direction.

The Danubian Countries

Rumania

Before the war Rumania, with a population of nearly 20 million people, was 110% self-sufficient, which means that 10% of its production was exported. A large part of those exports consisted of wheat, of which a record of 41 million bushels was shipped, as well as corn, barley and hogs. Farming, as in all Danubian countries, was on a very primitive level, but the soil is extremely fertile. Little fertilizer was used, and farm machinery was used only on large farms. Around 82% of the population was still living on farms.

During the war Germany saw to it that farm output was increased. Acreages planted to grain were well maintained and those of oilseeds increased.

Rumania lost the fertile provinces of Bessarabia and Northern Bukovina. Its urban population increased because many people from the lost provinces went to the capital, Bucharest, and to the other cities. In 1945 it experienced a very serious drought, and also because of the war, not all of the acreage was seeded. Further inroads into supplies were made by the Red Army's taking what it needed. In 1945/46 Rumania, therefore, was not able to export food, and its urban population lived under difficult conditions. The distribution of the available food was very unequal. Because few industrial goods could be bought, the farmers had no incentive to sell and were hoarding. While the peasants, who normally mainly ate corn, were eating white bread, the population of the cities got limited amounts of corn and had little white bread.

The crop, which is now being harvested, seems to be close to normal. The weather has been good, and the soil seems to have been fully cultivated. Exports of wheat and corn can be expected, the only question being whether they will go to the West or to Russia. Those exports should be relatively large, because the number of hogs and chickens, due to the bad harvest, is still below normal and more corn will be marketed as a result.

For these reasons we expect that the exportable surplus of grain (wheat, rye, barley and corn) will be 1–1.5 million tons. Whether Russia will claim deliveries on reparation account remains to be seen; for reasons outlined in the section on Russia, we do not expect this to be the largest part of the Rumanian exports, especially as long as the country needs foreign equipment for the reconstruction of its oil, lumber and other important industries.

Hungary

Hungary, with a prewar population of 8.5 million, was one of the richest agricultural countries before the way, exporting 18% of its production, the highest percentage in Continental Europe. Wheat, rye, oats, barley, corn and potatoes were the main crops, and while large amounts of wheat were exported, corn production was the basis of hog and poultry exports.

The land was to a great extent in the hands of big estate-owners, while most of the farmers were tenants. A large and unsystematic land reform program is taking place at present, and though a division of the great estates is called for, the peasants who are getting small farms do not have the needed equipment and livestock.

Hungary, more than any other country, is suffering from war requisitions. The Germans had removed most of the rolling stock, farm equipment and livestock. Some of what was confiscated is now held in the American zone of Germany. The Russians in turn not only lived off the country, but requisitioned food and farm equipment. The American government has just now accused them of doing so until at least last April.

With the Russians living off the land, a heavy drought decreased the crops. Cattle herds have been reduced to 30% of normal and hog holdings to even less. In all, Hungary has had a very difficult winter. The urban population, especially in Budapest, got only small rations and the situation was made worse by the greatest runaway inflation in history, which encouraged hoarding and maldistribution.

In spite of the lack of equipment, this fertile country will probably produce enough food this year to feed its population. The distribution, however, will remain unequal if inflation cannot be stopped. Hungary was to receive help from UNRRA, but as late as in June that help had only consisted of one million cans of fish, which were to be given to institutions and community kitchens.

Hungary has just made a very interesting proposal to UNRRA. It asked that organization in the coming year to provide it with the most necessary equipment, for which it would pay back from the proceeds of the coming harvests. However, UNRRA cannot make such an arrangement.

At present there is a tendency towards a long-run shift in farming from wheat to livestock production, since the wheat grown on small farms will probably not be able to compete with American and Canadian wheat. Whether there will be a greater market for livestock products, however, will first have to be worked out.

Bulgaria

Before the war, 79% of Bulgaria's 6 million population lived on farms. Of exports of agricultural products, however, only tobacco and prunes were of real importance. The country did not go through actual warfare, and farming this year can be expected to come up to prewar levels. Some exports of wheat, barley and fruit can be hoped for, but wheat exports never exceeded 8 million bushels. Whether these exports will go west or to Russia remains to be seen.

Great Britain

Food Minister John Strachey stated on July 3 that normal wheat consumption is at a rate of 100,000 tons a week (3.75 million bushels), which means 5.2 million tons or 195 million bushels a year. That would be less than in prewar times. Potato consumption, however, has risen by 61% since then.

British Bread Rationing: Why and How Long?[9]

The surprising bread rationing in Britain was explained on July 4th by the Minister of Food, John Strachey, by the fact that on request of the United States and especially the Hoover Committee, Great Britain had depleted herself of its bread grain reserve. Hoover's report indeed mentioned that England had released 11.25 million bushels of wheat from its stocks which were, so to say, "lent" and have to be given back to Great Britain by the United States. It has now only an eight-week supply, most of it in the necessary "pipe lines". Of this supply, as of July 31, 1946, 18.65 million bushels were in ships, warehouses and in transit,

---

The Requirements of the British Isles

The food situation of the United Kingdom before and after the war looks as follows, in millions of short tons:[8]

	Production			Domestic Production Avail. for Food		Net Imports	
	1934-38	1945/46* 1944		1934-38	1945/46*	1934-38	1945/46*
Wheat	1.9	3.5	2.4	0.7	2.0	6.1	3.6
Flour						0.5	0.5
Oats	2.2	3.6		0.1	0.2	0.1	0.1
Barley	0.8	2.3		0.6	1.1	1.0	0.1
Potatoes	5.5	10.9		4.0	7.9	0.2	
Corn							0.5
Meat	1.4	1.0		1.4	1.0	1.5	1.1
Fish (incl. canned)	1.1	0.9		0.2	0.2	0.14	

* Estimate

and 11.25 million bushels of flour in the mills. The prewar average volume carried at that time of year seems to have been 37-38 million bushels.

Strachey added that the United States had promised to send 5.6 million bushels of wheat to Britain in the next three months, and in addition to deliver 4.5 million bushels to the British zone in Germany. He revealed that England has sent since 1945

60,000	tons cereals, mostly wheat, to India	
60,000	tons cereals, mostly wheat, to Italy, Greece and Yugoslavia	
60,000	tons cereals, mostly wheat, to Germany outside the British zone	
192,000	tons wheat	
109,000	tons flour	to Germany's British zone, a total
105,000	tons barley	grain equivalent of about 450,000
132,400	tons potatoes	tons or 15.67 million bushels
718,400	tons total	

Strachey explained that British rationing was necessitated, aside from the low supply of reserves, by the fact that the Labor government could not rely on the hope that Canada would have a good wheat crop or that the United States would be able to ship the above quantities to Great Britain and the British zone of Germany during the coming three months, while the British Isles "would receive during August 11 million bushels, and during September 94 million bushels from their own harvest."

The impression obtained from Mr. Strachey's speech and the ensuing debate in the House of Commons on July 4, 1946 was that the American promises were not to be relied upon due to the uncertain labor relations and the unsettled price and delivery conditions in this country, and that the British government feared a late harvest in its own country. Great emphasis was laid on the necessity that the United States feed the British zone in Germany. In so far as the sensational British bread rationing had a foreign policy aim, it was evidently this.

The world trade statistics used by Strachey were identical with those of the FAO, but with evident skepticism as to the favorable crop news which must already have been known to his Ministry, and with doubt as to the ability of America to mobilize sufficient grain for exports, even if more or less promises.

It should be mentioned that the U.S. Department of Agriculture said on July 15th that 30 million bushels of wheat were at their disposal, of which 7.5 million bushels, or 200,000 tons, would be sent to England before September 1, and that this was the only commitment the government had toward the world. (The scheduled exports to India evidently are not "commitments".)

Astonishing as Mr. Strachey's doubts are, it shows that Great Britain is unable to bear the burden of food deliveries into its German sector, and desires that the United States do so—at least the actual deliveries, while the willingness to pay for it was not discussed in the debate. Since Great Britain has now contracted 160 million bushels of wheat from Canada for each of the next two years, it might in the future draw on Canada for its German zone.

Great Britain has made great efforts during the war to feed its own population. While rationing is functioning admirably, and the low-salaried people are sure to get their share and the necessary amount of calories, the food situation is far from good. Complaints about the monotony of the food are common. Fats, eggs, meat and fruits are scarce. The English housewives of all classes seem to be exhausted from their task. Reports from Belgium and Holland sound much more cheerful. The problem, however, is not one of available supplies only, but also of foreign exchange and price policy.

Before the war England was about 70% dependent on food imports. It received most of its food grain from overseas, and imported huge quantities of feed grains, oilseeds, livestock, products and fruits. During the war a large part of the pasture was plowed and cultivated for food grains. The number of hogs and poultry was reduced in order to devote as much acreage as possible to direct human food. The cattle herds, however, were not reduced, and the amount of milk in liquid form kept at a maximum. Great Britain actually achieved 50% self-sufficiency.

Since there was no anticipation of a wheat shortage, part of the crop land was reconverted to pasture in the fall of 1945 and the cultivation of feed grains. The goal for next year is a 10% higher wheat acreage. The prospects for the harvest are good, but the crops may be harvested late.

In early June the British government announced that feed rations will be greatly reduced from October 1946 to April 1947. There will be a planned decrease in livestock holdings, which will diminish meat and egg production. Even dairy cattle are to get lower rations, until more feed grain is available. Whether Great Britain will not reverse this policy if our corn crop turns out according to expectations, remains to be seen. At present it seems to be contracting oats from the United States.

The total import requirements of Great Britain for 1946/47 as anticipated by the FAO seems to be 6–6.25 million tons (220-240 million bushels) of wheat equivalent, including grains and all other food.

Eire

A small amount for Eire (Ireland) will have to be added to the British imports. Eire did not get an allocation for May -September 1946 by the Hoover Committee, and got along by raising the wheat extraction rate. Eire is exporting livestock products, mainly live cattle and eggs, to Great Britain. Though the crops are doing well, it may have to import 7–10 million bushels of wheat. Eire relies heavily on potatoes.

Middle East, South Africa and Latin America

In figuring its 30.5 million tons world import requirements of wheat and wheat equivalents for 1946/47, the FAO combines into one group those countries of the Middle East which were not directly involved in war: all of Africa except French North Africa and the entire Latin American world. To this large group of countries, together with the British Isles, the FAO assigns an import requirement of 8 million metric tons as mentioned above. As the British Isles will get 6–6.25 million metric tons of this total, the requirement for the remainder is put at only 1.75–2 million tons.

Of this, those Latin American countries, which are normally importers of cereals, are scheduled to buy about 1.5 million tons which is very close to their normal prewar import average. The needs of the Middle East and South Africa are figured at between 0.3–0.5 million metric tons cereal imports. The Middle East,

Turkey, Iran and Egypt are normally food exporters, especially of cereals on a considerable scale.

The Hoover Committee assigned for the months May–September 1946 to

Latin America	1 million tons of wheat or wheat equivalent		
The Middle East	0.1 million	"	"	"
Union of South Africa	0.2 million	"	"	"

All these figures are pretty close to the average imports of those regions in prewar years. They have been accepted for the purposes of this memo.

The very latest reports indicate such a good harvest result that the actual import needs may become lower than the 1.75 million metric tons, taken all together.

The Countries of the Middle East

Egypt

This country was in prewar times an exporter of rice and eggs. During the war cotton acreage was partly converted to food production; this improved the food situation so that it was better than in prewar times. Egypt is harvesting a bumper crop of rice and may export 200,000 tons of rice and sorghum, mainly to India.

Turkey

Before the war this country was an exporter of 750,000 tons of grain. It was badly hit by the drought last year, but for the year 1946/47 the prospects are excellent. While Bromhall's Corn Trade News (London) on July 26th estimates the possible export volume of grains in the range of 1–3 million tons (with a normal total average prewar production of 7 million tons), other reports, also of the U.S. Department of Agriculture, are less optimistic. Half a million tons may be a realistic appraisal.

Iraq

This country was, according to Hoover, able to "lend" about 200,000 tons of grain to India and some others. For 1946 the exportable surplus is lately estimated at 300,000 metric tons. (OFAR)

Syria and Lebanon

These countries will export about 50,000 tons of grain and 8,000 tons of olive oil.

Iran

This country has grain and dates for export.

Palestine

This country reports a fair citrus crop with 6.2 million cases to be exported, and also a good olive crop. Grain imports, however, may again amount to 100-150,000 tons.

Union of South Africa

Last year's drought was a disaster.

The Hoover Committee allocated 200,000 metric tons from May to September, but the country was able to buy 350,000 tons. The Union, nevertheless, will introduce bread rationing as of August 15, 1946. This decision was made on May 15 and the arguments were similar to those used by the British Food Ministry on July 4. It is now reported (OFAR on July 29) that the new grain crop will be almost double that of last year, and will therefore be "slightly above average". The reported deficiency is now mainly one of fats and oils. Import needs for wheat may remain below 100,000 tons for 1946/47.

Latin American Grain Importers

Latin America as a whole always exported large quantities of food, especially cereals, sugar and bananas. Some countries, however, are traditionally importers.

Cuba

This country will export about 50% more sugar than the 1936-40 average. The usual prewar imports consisted of rice and some wheat and flour. These imports may be about 250-335,000 metric tons in 1946/47. Because purchasing power has risen, the demand for food is greater.

Brazil

The average prewar imports of 0.9 million metric tons of cereals were offset last year by about 30% by a higher consumption of domestically grown corn and rice.

A very good crop in the current year has up to now kept imports of wheat and flour below the prewar average. However, this may change as soon as more grain becomes available. The exports of milled rice are expected to reach 335,000 metric tons, most of it in 1946.

Chile and Ecuador

These countries may export 100,000 metric tons of rice.

Peru

This country will again be an importer of wheat, wheat flour and rice to the extent of perhaps 100-200,000 metric tons of wheat equivalent.

Conclusion

We therefore find that the import needs of all this group of countries, aside from the British Isles, is no larger than their normal prewar average, and that they therefore are not putting any added strain on world supplies. We have also found some rather unexpected evidence of export surpluses in some Middle Eastern countries.

The Far East

The Rice Nations

For almost half of the world's population, rice is the mainstay of subsistence. Rice supplies 65–80% of the food requirements of the "rice nations", supplemented to a minor degree by some other cereals. Potato planting has been progressing lately in Japan, particularly under Axis influence. Nutrition from animal sources, except for fish, is much less important than in Europe and America, and dairy cattle, while of the greatest importance in India, is almost non-existent in such parts of the Far East as Japan.

The rice crop in the Far East is evaluated by the FAO as follows:

Rice Production in the Far East (Paddy Basis)
(in million metric tons)

Prewar average	140	(export surplus 3 million tons)
1945/46	118	(drought year)
1946/47 estimate	128	

The import needs of the Far East were almost entirely met by Taiwan and Korea for Japan, and for all other countries by Burma, Thailand and Indochina. Japan, which had become by far the greatest rice importer in the world, has lost its two suppliers of rice. Almost the whole Far East was hit by a heavy drought in 1945/46, and there was actual warfare in Thailand and civil war in Indochina.

Import Requirements in the 1946/47 Crop Year

Under the emergency conditions of this spring, the Hoover Committee defined the grain needs of the rice countries until the new harvest follows:

Allocations to the Far East by the Hoover Committee
Number of Grain Allocations May-September
(People 1946 in million metric tons)

India	248.7 million*		2.336
Ceylon	7.0	"	0.300
Malaya, etc.	3.6	"	0.250
Philippines	14.0	"	0.060
China	220.0	" *	0.870
Japan	75.0	"	0.870
Korea (U.S. zone)	4.0	"	0.110

Total 4.796
mill. metric tons

---

* Capacity of inland transportation

Because of the increased population, even to raise the per capita consumption of the Far East to a halfway satisfactory level would, according to the estimates of the FAO, require 11 million or at least 10 million tons of wheat during our 1946/47 crop year, as explained earlier in this report.

This latter figure, too, seems to us rather theoretical. *We believe that the actual amount which will be required, and which can be transported to the areas where it is needed, will not be higher than 7.5 million tons.* We arrived at this figure on the following basis:

In our 1946/47 crop year we will, first of all, have to take care of those Far Eastern food deficiencies which are a consequence of the below-normal crops of the winter 1945/46. Herbert Hoover has estimated grain requirements for May to September, which cover this period, at 4.8 million metric tons, of which little was shipped in May and June. His finding was verified in the case of the main recipient, India, by an American commission under the leadership of Dr. D. Theodore Schultz, which just returned from India.

Requirements during the later months of the crop year will be low until May or June, due to the new incoming harvests. If these harvests turn out better than this year, as can be safely expected, the requirements at the end of our 1946/47 crop year will be lower than this year. From October on to the end of June they may amount to 2.5 million tons.

The requirements as estimated by the FAO were lowered partly by the fact that higher exportable surpluses of rice showed up in Thailand and Indochina than was expected.

Lack of Transportation Limits Help

The actual need for imports will no doubt be higher than 7.5 million tons. Lack of transportation facilities into the interior, however, make more help from the outside impossible.

Herbert Hoover in his report on China stated that it will be impossible to reach most of the starving population in the interior because of the absence of transportation. In his opinion, about 800,000 metric tons, or 30 million bushels, is the maximum quantity of grain that can be moved into China in 1946.[10]

RICE

World Production and Distribution, 1936-1947, Statistics and Forecasts of the FAO

Thousand Metric Tons (paddy basis)

	Prewar			Area or Country	1945-46 (July-June)			1946-47 Production Forecast
	Production	Net trade (exports)	Disappearance		Production	Net trade (exports)	Disappearance[a]	
				A) FAR EAST EXPORTERS				
	17,900	-8,100	9,800	Burma, Thail., Indochina	10,900	-900[b]	10,800	13,300[c]
	5,500	-2,200	3,300	Korea, Taiwan	4,000	?	4,000	4,100
	23,400	**-10,300**	**13,100**	**Subtotals A)**	**14,900**	**-900**	**14,800**	**17,400**
				B) FAR EAST IMPORTERS				
	42,100	2,000	44,100	India	42,000	250	42,250	45,000
	12,100	2,400	14,500	Japan	8,000	?	8,000	9,200
	54,200	600	54,800	China and Manchuria	45,000	100	45,000	46,000
	9,000	1,200	10,200	Malaya, NEI & Philippin.	7,500	400	7,900	8,200
	300	800	1,100	Ceylon	200	300	500	300
	117,700	**7,000**	**124,700**	**Subtotals B)**	**102,700**	**1,050**	**103,650**	**108,700**

C) OTHER EXPORTERS							
U.S.A.	1,020	-150	870	1,430	-660	770	1,470
Egypt	650	-180	470	850	-250	600	800
Brazil and Chile	1,380	-40	1,340	2,120	-420	1,700	2,300
Italy and Middle East	1,450	-280	1,170	1,180	-50	1,130	1,300
Subtotals C)	**4,500**	**-650**	**3,850**	**5,580**	**-1,380**	**4,200**	**5,870**
D) OTHER COUNTRIES							
Europe and U.K.	310	2,050	2,360	300	—	300	300
North America & Cuba	290	450	740	410	360	770	410
Other Countries	2,050	1,350	3,400	2,300	—	2,300	2,300
Subtotals D)	**2,650**	**3,850**	**6,500**	**3,010**	**360**	**3,370**	**3,010**

[a] After stock changes.

[b] Almost all from accumulated stocks.

[c] Excludes old stocks yet to be shipped.

See also *Report on World Food Situation*, Technical Supplement 4, Commodities, p. 15, May 20, 1946.

UNRRA officials complain bitterly about inefficiency and waste in that country. Relief shipments are clogging the main ports and are not being distributed properly. Politics and graft are taking their toll.

Information which we obtained from Army headquarters in *Japan* showed very decided skepticism as to much help from the outside. On June 22 a letter from one of General MacArthur's aides said that Japan will either subsist on 65% of normal supplies or starve, as it is not expected that food imports into Japan proper will amount to anything substantial.

The Hoover Committee has allocated to Japan almost 800,000 tons (30 million bushels) of wheat, or wheat equivalent, until the new harvest which, though of no substantial help, may contribute toward overcoming actual starvation.

The Far East Normally a Surplus Area

Before the war the Far East not only equalized its own food deficits, but in addition exported 3 billion pounds of rice, 4 billion pounds of oilseeds and 2.3 million short tons of sugar to the Western world.

In spite of the huge food exports, *scarcity and famine were normal in parts of the Far East.* India and China have had their large share of it in various areas. In those two countries, with a total population of 850 million people, which is still increasing at a high rate, *famine will not be avoided until the farmers have learned to make better use of their soil and until transportation has been improved.*

In 1943, owing to a bad crop in Bengal, and due to the occupation of Burma by Japan, India lost 1,750,000 people through starvation. This cannot be allowed to happen again, nor will it. Unfortunately reports have just arrived from Bengal that the fear of shortages has led to heavy buying by a few grain dealers. The grain moved into their hands, grain prices are rising rapidly, giving rise to black marketeering, and in spite of supplies at hand, the poorer part of the population is starving. For these reasons a critical situation may develop although, according to OFAR, total food supplies are greater than in 1943.[11]

The Outlook Has Become Brighter

Since the FAO May report was written, favorable developments have improved the total aspect in the Far East.

OFAR in its new report, dated July 1, 1946, says:

Deaths from starvation have been much below expectations, indicating an efficient utilization of food supplies...If shipments can be maintained at the present levels, the increasing food supplies from domestic sources should be sufficient to relieve the present food crisis."

This may be contrasted with the dramatic appeal of the delegate from India on May 21:

A failure of these supplies will not only mean the threat of death for millions...(but) the entire foundations of a vast society will be shaken as they have never been shaken before."

The main events which have prevented starvation so far are:

1. In many parts of India *collections from previous years' harvests were above expectations,* and "total supplies have been sufficient to maintain the daily ration of one pound of cereals per person in most areas, and few deaths from starvation have been reported."

2. As mentioned before, surplus stocks of rice in Thailand, which were known to be there, showed up after the British government offered adequate and incentive payment. According to the 1945 armistice, Thailand had "to supply free of cost" rice up to 1.5 million tons. None appeared, so that in April/May, Lord Killearn bought 1.2 millions tons for £12/1/4 a ton, and paid a premium of £3 per ton on rice delivered up the end of May, and a premium of 2 shillings a ton from that date to June 15, 1946. Since then rice has been pouring out of Thailand, mostly to hungry India. In June the monthly rate of exports reached 60,000 tons. Some 100,000 tons for export seem to have been made available in southern Indochina. The Hoover Committee did not expect to get more than 400,000 tons out of both regions; in fact, it expected only 190,000 tons with certainty.

3. Imports of Rice from Brazil and other South American countries have been fairly substantial. Wheat has been shipped from Australia

4. Japan, with the help of the MacArthur administration, has started a campaign to help herself, which commands admiration.

5. In several countries, root crops and other quickly-maturing crops are being expanded.

The outlook for the 1946/47 crop year is better than for the previous year. *The rice acreage will be larger, though not up to normal,* since there is a serious lack of draft power and equipment in some parts, and prices for rice are uncertain because of political disturbances. Favorable reports indicating wheat and other winter crops much higher than in 1945, and probably not far below the prewar average, have arrived from northern China.

The total outlook for the new crop year, however, cannot be judged with any hope of accuracy until September or October, it being at least four months from now until the beginning of the harvest. However, it is certain that rice crops in the three main exporting countries—Burma, China and Indochina—could be much improved if cheap cotton goods and some simple farm equipment could be made available.

Little can be expected from either Korea or Taiwan. While those two countries provided Japan with as much as 1.7 million tons of rice, and Thailand provided Japan with sugar, in addition to exporting to other countries, both crops are expected to become much smaller under the Chinese administration, whose efficiency has yet to be proved. Any exportable surpluses of rice and sugar would go to China.

The Indian Subcontinent

The British Minister of Food in his memo on the world food crisis[12] reveals the following situation in India:

Of a population of 410 million, 70% are directly dependent on agriculture. The population is increasing at the rate of over 5 million a year, and food production is not keeping pace with this increase. Only a small part of the surplus from the millions of farms ever reaches the market.

India normally imported an average of 1.25 million tons of rice a year from Burma. When the Japanese conquered Burma this source of supply was cut off, and the result was a bad famine in Bengal in 1943. Since then the authorities in India have extended the acreage of food crops and introduced rationing in the large cities and many of the smaller ones. During 1943/44 and 1944/45 India had good harvests both of wheat and rice, but never enough to enable the authorities to build up working stocks.

In the late summer of 1945 a cyclone, a tidal wave, and in particular the general lack of rains, which normally occur during December/January on over much of India, resulted in a drop of 3 million tons below expectation in rice and millet crops. In addition, there was a very large deficit of 4-4.5 million tons in the expected crops of wheat, barley and grain to be harvested in the spring of 1946. The disastrous failure of the winter rains has caused India to increase its import requirements of cereals (wheat and rice) in 1946 from 1.5 million tons to over 4 million.

A closer collaboration of India's surplus provinces seems to have mobilized more rice for the "affected provinces" than the 200,000 tons which Herbert Hoover expected them to supply. Hoover allocated 2.34 million tons of grain to India for the period May to September. Until May 21, according to India's delegate, not more than 200,000 had arrived.

The Indian delegate at the FAO meeting in Washington complained bitterly about the *allocations made by the Combined Food Board*. While India had asked for 4 million tons of cereals in 1946, the Combined Food Board reduced this requirement to 1.4 million metric tons, of which the abovementioned 200,000 tons reached India toward the end of May.

The recently returned American Famine Mission to India, headed by Dr. Schultz, reported on July 25 that *the United States should export a minimum of 750,000 tons of wheat to India* with the greatest possible speed to prevent collapse of the rationing system. Secretary of Agriculture Anderson was quoted as saying that 500,000 tons of wheat are "in the cards" for India. Dr. Schultz also said that he would strongly urge the IEFC to set up *a 2 million ton world allocation of food for India*. In addition to the 750,000 tons from the United States, this would include 860,000 tons of rice from Java, Thailand, Burma and Egypt, corn from the United States and Argentina, and wheat from Australia.

The figure of 2 million tons ties in with the allocations of Mr. Hoover. In addition to the 200,000 tons, which had arrived by the end of May, another 200,000 tons may have been shipped to India by the second half of July. This leaves approximately 2 million tons still to be delivered.

This Indian delegate to the FAO meeting made the following very impressive statement:

> The people of the United States produce and consume 130 million tons of grain, compared with which my people, who are three times that number, consume only 60 million tons in normal times, and this year face a deficit of 7 million tons from that 60 million average.
>
> I do not want the Western world to go wholly vegetarian, but by becoming a little less non-vegetarian, they can find all the grain that is needed for feeding human beings numbering millions...and save them from the imminent threat of death by starvation."

The Japanese Food Problem

Japan's increasing scarcity of land has motivated its expansion since 1930. In fact, its soil did not yield more than 80% of its main food, rice. Conquered Korea, Taiwan and northern China had to make up for the rest. The nation was still growing during the war. In 1941 a population of 74 million on the Japanese islands and Taiwan was mentioned to us; the Allied Commander spoke recently of about 70 million, while the latest figure of the Japanese government is 77.1 million as of June 1946.

Information from knowledgeable persons who have just returned from Japan indicates that the situation there is bad, but not desperate. The collaboration with the Supreme Commander of the Allied Powers (SCAP) is evidently excellent, the more so since the Japanese do not expect too much from the outside, but have turned their energy toward solving their food problem with their own relatively poor soil by closer national collaboration.

A good deal of help from America will still be needed through 1946; less will be necessary in 1947. From 1948 on, if the prevailing efforts succeed, the country will not live on relief to any great degree.

During the Year 1946

Bad weather, disorganization resulting from the war, and the lack of supplies from Taiwan and Korea have created a serious food problem in 1946. As in most countries, serious hardship is prevalent in the big cities. Before the war, 50% of the population lived on farms. Many more have returned to them since, both because their urban homes were destroyed and because the government has advised the population to move to the country wherever possible to relieve the acute food situation in the cities, and to help till the soil.

Before the Hoover Committee was to make its decision, the Japanese government reported that it had only been able to collect 2.7 million tons of rice in the crop year beginning December 1945, that is 80.7% of its goal of 3.34 tons, whereas the crop harvested in 1945 had been 5.4 million tons of rice. This statement was evidently meant to impress the Committee.[13]

The allocation which Japan finally got was 0.87 million tons of wheat or wheat equivalent, of which not much had arrived in June. In July, for the first time, a 10-day supply to complete the rations of 67,500 tons was handed over by SCAP, plus 5,000 tons of military food which was in danger of spoiling on Iwo Jima.[14] If deliveries were to be continued at that rate, as they evidently will be, the Hoover schedule for 1946 will be filled.

Nevertheless, the Japanese are looking desperately for more expedients. One agency even reports a plan to buy rice at exorbitant prices on the black market—a grotesque idea indicating the scope of the difficulties.

The Situation in 1947

The Supreme Commander of the Allied Powers in Tokyo stated in his plan for 1946/47 that the "arable land of the Japanese homelands will produce only about 80% of the rice and 20% of the sugar that the population requires."

About 2 million tons of rice or other grains, he says, will have to be imported every year. He stressed the necessity of increasing the supply of chemical fertilizers.

This would indicate that in the coming year Japan will come close to its prewar indigenous rice production. The deficit amounts to what Korea and Taiwan sent to Japan. As military authorities generally have a tendency not to minimize the requirements of their territories, it will probably be possible to cut this deficit. Moreover, Japan can count on an increase in its production through the help of a large shipment of fertilizers, which is to come from the United States, and which is part of the allocation of 350,000 tons for Germany and Japan combined.

The Japanese fertilizer industry is partly destroyed. In May 1946, the industry produced only one-third of its prewar output.[15] A "fertilizer council", collaborating with SCAP, has drafted an Emergency Fertilizer Plan, and the aim is production of 260,000 metric tons of pure nitrate content by July 1947. Phosphates will be made available.[16]

Land Reforms

Under the necessity of living on less soil, the Japanese together with SCAP have drafted a five-year land reclamation program.[17]

This is the program:[18]

Proposed in five years (April 1945–March 1950): reclamation of 3.8 million acres.

To be completed in time for planting in 1946: 0.33 million acres.

To be completed on January 31, 1946: 0.09 million acres.

In addition, a land reform is scheduled. A large proportion of the tenant farmers, who work two-thirds of the total farm land, are to become owners.

Switching to Potatoes

Under the influence of German agronomists, the Japanese have been switching from rice to potatoes, also to sweet potatoes, as illustrated by the graphs on the two following pages.

Japan's Second Food—Fish

Next to rice, fish is Japan's most important food. Fish is not only a substitute for meat, but also a source of fat. We can help a good deal to take Japan off relief by re-establishing Japan's fishing industry. In 1940 that country had more than 354,000 fishing vessels totaling 1.1 million gross tons. Of these about one-third were destroyed in the war. News which we have received shows that production may come up to the rate of the prewar catches of 3 million tons per year by the end of 1946. But Japan has to increase its output of fish, and in this matter the Japanese are really hopeful. The Russians, impressed by the difficult food situation, have allowed Japanese fishing along their territory in Korea and on Sakhalin. Whaling has been allowed to them in the Bonin Islands.

Four Major Food Crops in Japan
1926–1945

WHEAT

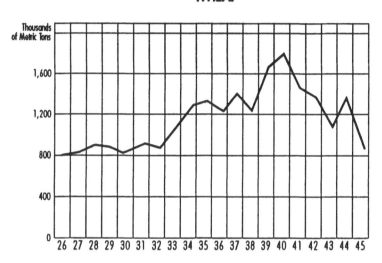

SWEET POTATOES

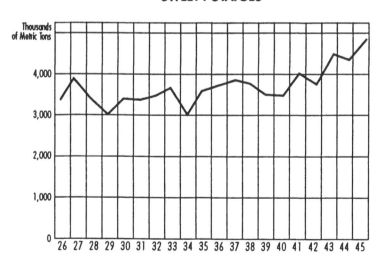

Source: General Headquarters—Supreme Commander for the Allied Powers —1946.

Four Major Food Crops in Japan (continued)

RICE

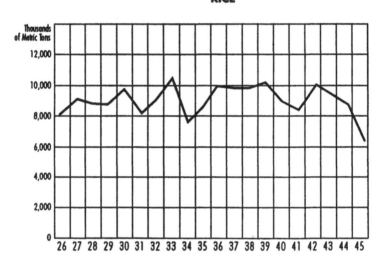

POTATOES

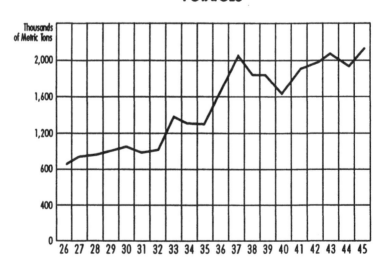

On American advice, the Japanese Bureau of Fisheries will build 1,214 steel fishing vessels; work has begun on 416, as well as on a number of wooden vessels.

Exports Scheduled to Buy Food and Raw Materials

The SCAP plan for the future is to have Japan export $400 million worth of commodities. In the 1935/39 period Japan exported about $464 million per annum. The aim of SCAP seems relatively high, but the total impression gained from a detailed report is that the Japanese are going to the task of reshuffling their economic structure with the greatest of energy. They will certainly live on smaller rations than in prewar times for years, but they will not starve, nor stay on relief as Germany inevitably must do.

The Philippines

The situation in that country of 14 million people is perhaps best characterized by the fact that while it used to be one of the world's largest sugar exporters, with an average export of 188,000 metric tons a year, during the last six months it urgently applied for 15,000 tons of sugar to be exported *from* the United States, and just got 5,000 tons from Cuba.

However, one of one of the other great export industries of the Philippines, copra, is already recovering. Shipments of copra for the 1946/47 season are expected to amount to 750 million pounds, as before the war. The oil mills, which formerly produced an average of 226,000 tons of coconut oil per year, were largely destroyed in the war.

Rice planted in century-old irrigation systems, as a rule, was not entirely sufficient to feed the population, but net imports before the war were only 57,000 tons. The war devastated the country, and drought further cut production. There were no civilian goods to be bought, so that farmers had no incentive to increase production.

The country called for an allocation of rice from the CFB at a rate of 20,000 tons a month, and for 3,500 short tons of meat. The Hoover Committee allocated 12,000 tons of wheat and wheat equivalent per month from May to September 1946.

Now the acreage of food crops, especially rice, is being increased, although it is still only 90% of the prewar acreage due to a shortage of carabao buffaloes and agricultural implements. But progress with others is slow, as shown by the figures of the sugar industry: prewar production in short tons was 1.12 million; in 1945, 12,500 tons, or a little more than 1% of prewar production; and in 1946 it will perhaps be 90,000 tons or 8% of prewar production.

The fishing industry has lost much of its equipment, but is now increasing its equipment to make up for meat, production of which is still said to be only 50% of prewar.

Imports of civilian goods, which will stimulate farm and factory output, are urgently needed on all sides. A special effort in that direction might stimulate food production and our political strength in this independent republic.

Notes

1. Report of the Special Meeting, FAO, Washington, D.C., June 6, 1946.
2. OFAR World Food Prospects for 1946/7, p. 6.
3. Release from the Office of Military Government for Germany (U.S.), Public Relations Service, Berlin, April 13, 1946.
4. See *The Economist*, April 6-20, 1946 (series of five articles).
5. With reference to Germany see also: Alvin Johnson and Ernest Hamburger, *The Economic Problem of Germany*, published in *Social Research*, June 1946, Vol. 13, No. 2.
6. Report in *Neue Zürcher Zeitung*, Zürich, Switzerland, May 2, 1946.
7. Russia's claim against Rumania is $300 million, payable in six years in petroleum, grains, machinery and some other commodities. Owing to the bad crop last year, the delivery of grains was delayed. Russia is in the long run interested in the reconstruction of the Rumanian economy. It has similar claims against Hungary, but here the caretaker interest—at least as far as is visible—now is much less.
8. See OFAR, *World Food Situation 1946*, p.82.
9. See record of food rationing debates in the House of Commons, July 4th and 19th; also based on impressions of British economists.
10. See also the unusually comprehensive report of China's Food Minister, Hon Kan, in *The China Magazine* of June 1946, which shows the enormous difficulties the Chinese government has to organize the exchange of food between parts of that giant country. Hon Kan figures that the Chinese rice crop of 1945 was 12% below prewar, while Taiwan's crop was 45% lower.
11. OFAR, *Foreign Agricultural Circular*, July 29, 1946.
12. *The World Food Shortage*, cmd. 6785, London, 1945, p. 7.
13. Memo from General Headquarters, June 1946. (In July the collections reached 80% of the "quota", according to the Japanese Radio Home Service, July 23, 1946.)
14. *The New York Times*.
15. *Too Nippon*, June 6, 1946.
16. General Headquarters memo, June 3, 1946, and special report.
17. *Nippon Times*, June 15, 1946.
18. Japanese Ministry of Agriculture and Forestry, March 1946. The plan seems now to be tried on a much larger scale, as reported by the Japanese Radio Home Service on June 24, 1946.

Chapter FIVE

Important Food Stuffs Other Than Grain: Animals, Meat and the Problem of Maximum Prices

America's Meat Animals are Decisive for the World Food Supply

The importance of animal feeds for the world food problem has been shown here at length before. We do not see how our world rescue work in the spring of 1946 would have been possible if at that moment the United States would not have had 120 million hogs as in 1942-43, and instead only, say, 80 million. In a period of threatening scarcity of human food, the control of livestock and its feed becomes a duty of the first order.

The Animals Go West

This is also valid for America, though because of the war America has greatly increased its livestock, while those of the other continents, especially Europe, have decreased. This shift is of great importance (see charts).

While this decrease of livestock in Europe caused a scarcity of meat and dairy products which can only be made good over several years, the United States nevertheless has not felt a surplus

112

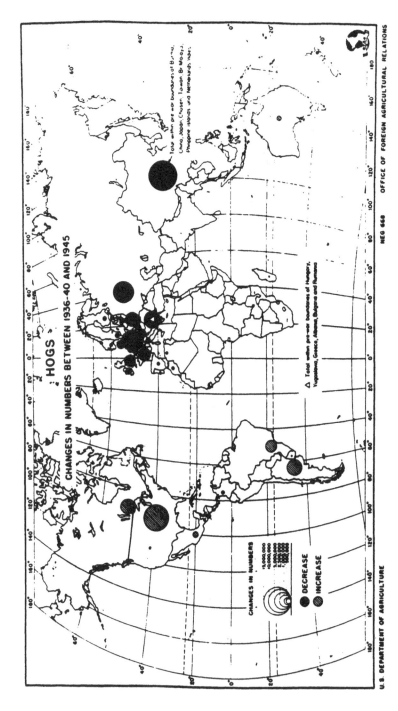

There were about 254 million head of hogs in the world at the beginning of 1945 compared with a 1936–40 average of 284 million. Further sharp declines have been experienced in central and southeastern Europe since the beginning of 1945.

several years, the United States nevertheless has not felt a surplus of meat. On the contrary, America's meat consumption has constantly risen and when there was not enough meat from cattle and hogs, chickens had to fill the gap.

When in the spring of 1946 the sudden world food scarcity arose, the tendency of USDA necessarily was to keep the number and weight of livestock down. USDA recommended that 10% fewer pigs be farrowed for the fall crop, and this advice was followed in such a way that the fall pig crop is expected to be 16% lower than last year. This, however, happened also for the reason that a keen shortage of feed grains was felt in the spring. Slaughtering decreased even more because the sellers expected the lifting of maximum prices.

According to the intentions of the farmers, as surveyed by USDA, the next coming spring crop, too, should be lower than it was last spring. It is doubtful, however, that that will really turn out to be the case and that the spring crop of hogs will be less than 52-53 million, for the new corn crop is expected to be large.

What Will Be the Effect of Possible Maximum Prices after August 20?

Resuming meat rationing is out of the question. The development of sophisticated black market techniques alone makes it impossible.

Maximum prices can be reinstated from August 20 on grains as well as on meat. Even if this should happen, we do not expect any great effect on the volume of livestock holdings and meat production.

USDA looks at the consequences of such a tendency as follows:[1]

> The principal uncertainty in the outlook for meat prices is the extent to which retail prices of other commodities and services will rise. If price control should be continued on most items important in the cost of living except meat, the general level of consumer prices would rise only moderately. In that event, part of the demand for meat would be transferred to relatively lower-priced foods and to other commodities; the price of meat at retail in October-December, on the basis of past relationships,

would be 15-20% higher than in June. On the other hand, if price controls are not restored and if the consumer price index should rise by as much as 20%, past relationships indicate that the average retail price of meat in October-December would be around 35% higher than in June.

Other factors that will affect the price of meat in the fall and early winter include changes in real income of consumers and in the supply of meat. Although income is rising, it is not likely to rise much faster than prices. The supply of meat per person during the fourth quarter of 1946 will be 18-20% larger than in the spring and summer, although 8-10% smaller than the very large amount available last fall when slaughtering was at a near-record level. Army contracts were being cancelled, and little meat was procured for export.

Production of meat for the year as a whole may be around 22.6 billion pounds (wholesale meat basis), compared with 22.9 billion pounds in 1945 and the record high of 24.7 billion in 1944.

While it does not say so openly, it is evident that USDA is of the same opinion about the efficiencies of price ceilings as we are. Even if artificial attempts at imposing maximum prices should be made, the actual price, especially for meat, would be to a large extent immediately determined by the black markets. Maximum prices for livestock would immediately drive the meat animals to non-federally-inspected packers, and the meat to the black market.

Possible maximum prices for grains—which at the moment do not seem probable—without maximum prices for meat would strongly favor overfeeding.

Such a system would not be tenable for any considerable period. As the Office of Price Administration (OPA) is no longer responsible for maximum prices, but because it and the USDA are usually blamed for food scarcities, we consider it very probable, in fact almost certain, that during most of the winter we will have free prices on grains and meat.

In particular, there are the following reasons for this belief:

Spring, Fall, and Total Pig Crops, United States, 1924–46

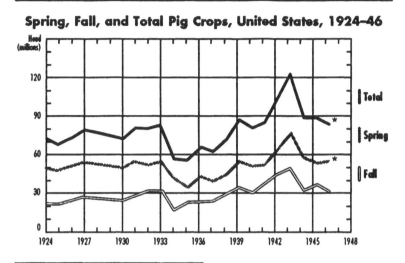

*Fall pig crop based on sows indicated to farrow and 1935–44 average number of pigs saved per litter.

Breeding intention reports on June 1 indicated that around 4.6 million sows would be bred for fall farrow this year, a decrease of 16 percent from a year earlier. This number is 39 percent below the 1943 record, 9 percent below the 1935–44 average and the smallest since 1938.

Since July 1, prices of corn have increased relatively more than hog prices and the hog-corn price ratio continues distinctly unfavorable to hog producers.

Source: U.S. Department of Agriculture.

USDA hopes that free markets will automatically bring a grain-to-animal ratio which will prohibit excessive feeding.

Secretary Anderson personally hopes that meat consumption will be somewhat reduced when increasingly more durable consumer goods become available again.

Even if this should not be the case, USDA always has possibilities of influencing price interrelations through the CCC.

USDA's forecast, that in 1946/47 we will have about the same quantity of meat as we had last year, will therefore probably be borne out.

Less Meat Overseas than Before
—How Much Feed?

For Europe, the most recent reports are:

In 1945 Europe, including England but excluding Russia, had 35% fewer hogs than prewar, and 13% fewer cattle. In addition, the cattle were of lower weight. England had about 75% of its prewar meat consumption, while consumption on the Continent as a whole seems to have been two-thirds or normal.

Indigenous meat production and imports into Europe are reported and forecast by USDA as follows:

Meat Production and Imports in Europe
(in billions of pounds)

	Production		Net Imports	
	United Kingdom	Continental Europe excluding USSR	United Kingdom	Continental Europe excluding USSR
Prewar	2.6	24.1	3.4	23.7
1945/46	2.1	13.2	4.6	0.8
1946/47	2.1	13.0	3.8	1.7

It is anticipated that meat exports will look as follows:

Exports of Meat
(in billions of pounds)

Country	Prewar	1945	1946
United States	–	1.2	1.3
Canada	0.2	0.8	0.7
South America	2.0	1.9	2.1
Australia, New Zealand and Denmark	3.7	5.5	5.7

For our consideration the result is this: less livestock than prewar on the European Continent requires fewer—far fewer—imports of feeds than prewar. The desire, however, is strong in most European countries to rebuild the livestock, especially the dairy cattle.

The practical question, however, will be who will have the needed dollars, and other foreign currency—and where and how much will those who don't have it, borrow.

Fish

Fish represent a potential additional food supply of large proportions. Because of enforced conservation during the war years, fish are more plentiful than ever.

The problems involved in making this food available in increased quantities to food-deficient countries are twofold. First is the need of rehabilitating the fishing industry, many boats of which, including their fishing gear, were lost during the war. This applies especially to the Mediterranean countries, Poland and Japan.

Those losses are now being made up, and the increased size of the catch is helping to make up for the deficiency of equipment. Thus we find the Norwegian delegate to the FAO explaining that his country delivered 750,000 tons of fish to Europe this year. The Danish delegate to the FAO offered one million kilograms more fish every week than sold now, if only payment could be found; and Sweden wants nothing more than to increase its fish exports.

This brings up the second and more difficult problem of making fish available to deficiency areas.

Fresh fish must either be iced or frozen, or be salted, dried, canned, or processed in some other way in order to make them available fit for human consumption at some distance from the seacoast. Here lack of labor and facilities have already proven to be a handicap in such countries as the United Kingdom and Norway; and even where processing facilities are available, transportation must be provided.

The latter problem exists no matter where food must be shipped, and the provision of supplies needed for pickling, salting and smoking, to say nothing of canning, would seem to be much more efficient and economical than the direct shipping of other food products from greater distances.

It is, in fact, admitted that liberal supplies of fresh fish can be made available to all areas within a short distance of the seacoast. It is not clear why Poland and Germany should be denied fish because they lack the money to pay for it. If they must be fed, it is obviously more economical to do so from a source of supply close to their borders than with grain shipped from the Dakotas and western Canada. It seems certain that some method of payment could have been arranged, and it is doubtful that the Swedish fishing industry or government would have insisted on exorbitant prices.

As an indication of the quantities of fish which will actually be at Europe's disposal, the FAO estimates that 400 million pounds of pickled herring will be available in 1946/47 as compared with only half of that quantity last year. In addition, there will be 308 million pounds of salt cod—again almost double the 1945/46 supply—and 492.2 million pounds of canned fish.

This alone makes a total of 1.2 billion pounds, to say nothing of the fresh or frozen fish which could be eaten by those living within reasonable distances from the coast.

The Far East

The situation in the Far East is clear. In China 50,000 fishing boats were lost during the war, while about one-third of all Japanese shipping was destroyed.

The occupation authorities in Japan are making every effort to restore the local fishing industry as rapidly as possible. Landing craft have even been turned over to the Japanese, and the occupation authorities expect to make the Japanese at least self-sufficient in this respect.

For China, UNRRA is making every effort to provide boats and equipment. Arrangements are also being made to procure dry-salted herring in British Columbia for shipment to China.

In addition to the above, Russia has given Japan permission to use its fishing grounds off Sakhalin, and only boats and equipment are needed to bring in a supply abundant enough to make up at least a considerable part of Japan's present rice deficiency.[2]

Fats and Oils

World supplies of fats and oils will be lower than in prewar times in the crop year beginning July 1, 1946, but they will be larger than in the previous crop year. In fact, from January 1947 on, the situation should be greatly eased.

While our own production of fats and oils will be somewhat lower than last year, due mainly to a decrease in soybean acreage, production in Europe will be greater, though still approximately one-third below prewar levels. The second great export area, Africa, will come close to exporting its prewar level of 2 billion pounds, and South America may even export more than its prewar figure of 1.6 billion pounds, shipping less linseed but much more sunflower seed oil.

Exports from Asia, which is the main exporting area, will still be considerably lower than in normal times, when they amounted to 4 billion pounds. They are, however, distinctly on the increase, even if the disorganization and dislocations arising out of the war in the Far East will prevent a sudden return to normal exports. The outlook for these exports is much brighter than could be hoped only a few months ago, with the exception of palm oil shipments from Java and Sumatra, and soybeans from Manchuria.

The FAO estimated the average annual world production at 27 billion pounds during the years 1935-39, while in 1945, the most unfavorable year, only 21 billion pounds were available. World exports before the war amounted to 11.7 billion pounds, but were down to 4.4 billion in 1945.

For all export areas, the following factors will relieve the supply picture:

1. Shipments of copra for the 1946/47 season from the Philippines will be up to the prewar level of 750 million pounds.

2. The Dutch East Indies will probably ship 350 million pounds—half of their prewar level.

3. Whale oil from the Antarctic will in 1945/46 amount to about 320 million pounds. For 1946/47 it is conservative to expect at least 620 million pounds, as compared with about 1,100 million pounds during the prewar period. If the international convention restricting production of whale oil is set aside, and the necessary ships are built, then considerably more whale oil may be expected. At present only nine factory-type ships are available as compared to more than 30 before the war. Sweden ordered building of one or two factory ships of its own.

4. Argentina's flaxseed exports will increase greatly in 1946/47. A new high price has been set by the Argentinean government which will expand acreage. Furthermore, there will probably be

a cessation of the withholding policy which cut world supplies in 1945/46.

5. Tung oil will become available from China.

On the basis of these factors alone, supplies of fats and oils will increase from these areas by about 1.5 billion pounds more than during 1945/46. This amount will go a long way toward reducing the world-wide deficit. While European production will remain below prewar levels in 1946/47—mainly because of the long period needed to build animal herds—European import needs (excepting Germany) will be considerably smaller than during 1945/46.

Sugar

Sugar was the first commodity to show surpluses on a world-wide basis. After the first attempts at internationally planned export restrictions in 1902, almost every year has brought a new plan for international sugar regulations.

During 1945/46 there was a decided shortage of sugar. World production had dropped from 34.5 million to 27 million short tons, due to a decrease of 5.3 million tons, or more than half of the prewar production in Europe; and to an almost complete lack of production in Java, the Philippines and Taiwan, which formerly exported 1.2 million tons, 0.9 million tons and 1.1 million tons, respectively. These increases were offset only partly by higher production in Cuba.

Production will be greater this year by about 3 million tons, since the increase in Europe is estimated to be approximately 1.5 million tons over last year. Cuba will be able to export 1 million tons more, and there will be sizable increases in Puerto Rico, Hawaii and Mauritius.

These new reports, contrary to the *Report on the World Food Situation* of the FAO dated May 20, show a decided increase in sugar supplies over the next years. In France, Italy and Spain good sugar harvests are expected. Czechoslovakia is already on an export basis. The main European deficits will be in Germany, Austria and Poland. The need for imports into Continental Europe will therefore be lower than last year, though we expect actual shipments to be somewhat higher.

Of the 4.5 million tons which the world will produce less than in prewar times, 1.1 million tons, which came from Taiwan, went to Japan. Japan will have to do with less sugar.

With 1.5 million tons more to be produced in the Caribbean area, it is quite conceivable that 1 million tons more will be allocated to the United States this year.

The fact that sugar production has increased in Europe is important for the demand of wheat, because the caloric value of sugar is very high and can only be made up through a higher consumption of cereals.

Notes

1. U.S. Department of Agriculture, Bureau of Agricultural Economics, *Livestock and Wool*, July 1946, pp. 4-5.
2. See the section on Japan.

Chapter SIX

Recommended Policies

Assumptions

While we assume no decisive influence of price control over food and feeds, we expect the present powerful influence of the USDA to continue. We also expect that present predictions of bumper crops in grains and feeds will be realized.

Recommendations

The policies here recommended cover three interrelated fields of action:

1. *Publicity and Propaganda*

The food scare propaganda which has proved unable to overcome the food crisis, but which may be used to force an internationally controlled egalitarian economy on the world, must be vigorously and skillfully met and overcome. Definite suggestions are given below.

2. *A Foreign Food Policy*

3. *A Federal Food Policy*

The policies to be followed by U.S. agriculture must be clearly defined and carefully coordinated. A list of general objectives and definite proposals has been outlined. With these objectives and proposals, your industry should ally itself not only through the weight of its public influence, but by its specific contributions to the country's need for food and feed concentrate as we have suggested.

As the volume of grains and most other foods will be sufficient to avoid any real scarcity in this country, and to allow for exports even higher than those scheduled by USDA in May, the psychological factor may become decisive.

If people are told that there will be scarcities, this alone may have adverse effects, as seen by bread hoarding and the farmers' strike in June 1946.

The fight-the-famine propaganda, which was aimed at a voluntary decrease in our food consumption and probably had to be tried out, had little positive effect. The food and money collections for overseas had little success up to now, and much less advantage than was expected was taken of the well-publicized opportunity of sending army surplus food to private people through a non-profit organization.

This propaganda, however, did have the consequence of bringing about the impression among farmers that their production would be needed for a long time. This has merely helped to raise prices, to encourage hoarding and to diminish supplies on the open markets.

Therefore the line followed by government publicity is of paramount importance. Even if crops are plentiful and if, as we showed, the European situation greatly improves, such speeches as the one Secretary of Agriculture Wallace delivered on July 15 will still give the impression of real scarcities. He spoke about 150 to 200 million people in Europe whose nutrition is below the standard necessary for health.

England and most of Continental Europe is, however, just now emerging from either scarcity or a very monotonous diet. Their views of the situation will always be more gloomy than those of a neutral observer who sees that conditions are improving worldwide.

Our occupation forces are necessarily very much inclined toward emphasizing the needs of the areas under their command. In June, Colonel H. B. Hester, Chief of the Military Government Food and Agricultural Branch in Germany, went so far as to claim that in order to improve the bad nutritional standards in occupied Germany, the United States should introduce bread rationing at home. He was impressed by the malnutrition which prevailed and the time and did not consider that things will look different after the new harvest. Similar sentiments and tendencies will undoubtedly be greatly strengthened by the coming meeting of the FAO in Copenhagen in September 1946, which will get a good deal of publicity, at least outside of America.

To anyone who is interested in getting our food economy back to normal, *it will be of great importance to observe these trends and to influence them as far as possible.*

A well-planned publicity campaign should emphasize the great improvement in the domestic and world food situation. Any threat or bogey of a possible new emergency will encourage hoarding by producers and speculators.

How to Fight the Food Scare Propaganda

1. Ensure that the true facts concerning the greatly improved crop conditions, not only in this country but also abroad, are given full publicity.

2. Check all claims of food shortages and starvation, and take necessary steps to see that the public, both here and abroad, is acquainted with the facts.

3. Expose the true aims of prolonged world food planning as the imposition of an internationally controlled egalitarian economy, for which the United States would be expected to pay the bill.

4. Beware of "requirement" statistics compiled only on the preliminary claims of governments fearing deficits. Always remember that the Hoover Committee had to "deflate" such requirements in the spring of 1946 by almost two thirds.

5. Publicize the increased productivity of American agriculture and draw attention to the inevitable coming danger of postwar surpluses.

6. Demonstrate that only through the return of free markets can all people get their fair share of the world's goods.

7. Announce that your own industry neither requires nor desires food grains, and publicize the importance the concentrates you produce have as cattle feeds.

8. Prepare all other steps necessary to forestall renewed food scare propaganda, which will undoubtedly be disseminated at the September meetings of the FAO and UNRRA.

Our Food Policy Abroad

Our leading slogan should be *Help the Food Deficit Nations to Help Themselves!* We start from the assumption that our food exports will be guided more by the idea of stopping shipments on a charity basis, than to provide everything for everyone everywhere. The means within our reach to achieve this are not only membership in the IEFC, FAO, UNRRA and other international agencies, but also our own policy concerning loans to foreign countries, and our collaboration in the international financial organizations such as the International Monetary Fund and the International Bank.

When drafting our general food policy for Europe, some special European needs and contradictory interests in Europe should not be overlooked.

We Pay Food to Germany to Satisfy Russia

We should be aware of the fact that we paid Russia for its enormous war effort by agreeing that she will get all the formerly Polish provinces east of the Curzon Line. We agreed to pay Poland by giving it 24% of the most fertile German crop land. This, in itself, means that *we took over the burden of sending a considerable amount of food to Germany* for a number of years, and it was evident from the first moment that Russia would not pay for it, nor contribute to maintaining a standard of living in Germany as outlined in the Potsdam Agreement of August 1945.

The change in the situation is that Great Britain feels herself unable to supply its German zone with its own food supply and that of Canada. Inevitably this food deficit for Germany, be it against loans or gifts, will have to be made up by America. The inability of Great Britain to fulfill these requirements was one of the paramount causes of the British bread rationing, and is now one of the major motives pushing toward unification of the non-

Soviet zones in Germany, and toward reestablishment of such German industries which should have been eliminated according to the original Potsdam plan.

This has made some of the most anti-German American officials in our occupation zone decided adherents of a unified Reich.

This obligation to feed Germany may be felt as a serious burden for a year or so. As soon as surpluses show up again, this phase of the matter will certainly not prove important.

There is one specific fear expressed by leading military officers who were stationed in Germany:

They expect the Russians to withhold exports of food surpluses from their zone in Germany to the other German zones. The hope is that after a while the Russian zone will be so well provided that the others might also long to come under the food conditions of Russian rule.

The speculation behind this is again that Great Britain had great difficulties in maintaining even a 1000-calorie diet. The Russians are aware of the fact that the Americans can and will do much better; but they expect a repetition of 1919-21: that the United States, tired of the incessantly growing claims that we alone feed the beaten enemy, may lose interest in Europe and more or less retire from it.

These viewpoints are being brought forward by persons of the highest competence.

There are some very evident divergences of interest in food policy between the various European nations:

Denmark, Holland and Switzerland (with New Zealand joining in) complain that America and Canada, by expanding cattle holdings and supplying England and others with dairy products, have begun to destroy the whole division of labor. Their ardent desire is to rebuild their dairy and meat animal industries. For this reason they would like to shift back from extensive food growing to more pasture and feed crops. But now is too early for that.

Therefore, we should encourage and demand a policy *gaining as much as possible from Europe's own soil in the coming year.* In fact, Belgium, Holland and France have already derived great benefits from this tendency.

When discussing these plans, we should never forget that the international division of labor has enriched all countries, and that there is no sense in striving to make them all self-sufficient. It will be expedient for us to have outlets for our own agriculture when the food crisis is over and forgotten. We must take care not to hamper our own industries unnecessarily by our actions to help others to help themselves.

Grains other than wheat should be stressed as food in Europe during 1946/47. Most of the nations have used potato flour with their bread. Corn and oats were always normal bread grains in some parts of Europe, and barley was used as an admixture. There is no reason why this should be different now.

Duties on such foods as corn flakes in Switzerland should be discouraged in times of corn abundance.

The general basic ideas for our food policies abroad can be outlined as follows:

Let us send means of food production rather than food. The most important help in this direction is *chemical fertilizers.* We refer to the appendix on chemical fertilizers, which shows the enormous possibilities which these fertilizers, after some years, will have in wiping out scarcities.

We should do all that we can to increase the production of those fertilizers in foreign countries which will not be able finance food imports in the near future. Some 80% of German chemical fertilizer production capacity is located in the Russian zone. Not only should this capacity escape destruction—it is provided for in the Allied plan for Germany that they have to be maintained, but every additional piece of machinery that enables the fertilizer plants to produce more will probably save its cost 20–100 times over in terms of needed food which we would then not have to send.

Japanese efforts to reestablish their formerly well-equipped fertilizer industry should be speeded up. Large supplies of phosphate rock are found in the Pacific. Transportation difficulties can be overcome.

The fertilizer industry should get high priority for coal in all food deficit countries, especially also in those occupied by the Allies.

Draft animals, agricultural implements and machinery— UNRRA has developed a very good understanding of these problems during the years of its existence.

American observers are inclined to underestimate the great importance of draft animals in all European countries. Americans, Canadians and Australians have learned to think in terms of tractors rather than of horses. In all European countries the horse is the normal tractor, and the mechanization of draft power is almost nowhere very far advanced. Even cattle are used to pull the plow. If horses can be made available in Europe, they should be used, but transportation of horses overseas usually entails considerable losses.

As to agricultural implements, UNRRA has emphasized that very low-grade agricultural tools are lacking throughout the Far East and in many other deficit countries. Sickles and hoes are needed in large quantities.

Whatever can be spared in old but still usable agricultural implements should also be sent to these countries. It would not even matter if some repairs would have to be made, though these would best be made in the country of origin. The war has taught many nations a lot in simple engineering.

UNRRA has tried to help the food deficit nations help themselves by various other methods. It quotes the following cases in which it was able to increase the food production of China: by installing several thousand blacksmith shops, 19 foundries and machine shops and one central specialized shop; by plants for manufacturing fertilizers and pesticides; and yards for making fishing boats. Most important of all: a great effort in controlling flooding of the Yellow River is now under way.

Large U.S. Loans as a Means of Increasing Food Supplies

An important factor are the loans which we are going to give in large amounts during the next two years. The figure which we published as to the probable size of these foreign payments reached $27-28 billion. This figure was exceeded some time ago by the U.S. Department of Commerce. While we only considered those loans and other money investments abroad to be given through the Bretton Woods organizations, the occupation armies and the Export-Import Bank, the Department of Commerce added some additional billions for private credits likely to be extended, and their final total was $30 billion to be given over several years.

As almost all of these loans have to be given under the auspices of the United States, or by international organizations which ultimately rely financially mainly or exclusively on the United States, we should be able to direct the use of these loans so as to increase food production power to make our debtors as self-sufficient as is technically possible and economically expedient.

It is imperative that the work of organizations like UNRRA, FAO, the Export-Import Bank, the International Fund and the International Bank be closely coordinated in order to avoid doubling of the loans, to supervise a reasonable use of our money and to maximize the effectiveness of these loans.

General Advice Concerning Agriculture

Intermediary crops, where possible, will be badly needed over all of Europe for more than a year. The influence of our occupation authorities should be directed along this line.

The tendency toward feeding roots instead of grain is in the direction of modern land use. The shift from grain to root crops can still be increased in Central Europe. For the next years it will be in their interest not only to maintain, but partly to expand these methods, especially as long as oilcakes will not be available to the extent they were before the war.

Soil Reclamation—For the Germans the main hope of getting farther toward self-sufficiency, and not to be a burden on the victorious nations, is to produce much more from the soil which is left to them. Within the borders of Germany there is still a considerable area which can be use taken into use, namely the Lüneburg Heath and probably considerable areas of forest land. Danish and American experts have developed devices which should be put into practice during this year, or at the beginning of next year. It may even be expedient to explore how far Dutch methods, which won provinces out of the sea, can be applied in Germany. The help we gave them in this would only relieve us of the cost of direct relief which we are bound to pay during the coming years.

It is worth mentioning again that the division of Germany into four zones dangerously reduces the possibility of feeding the Germans from their own soil. It is imperative to organize these parts of Germany at least so that the food and feeds production can be gotten from the reduced acreage.

Send *cotton goods* and other civilian goods, such as agricultural implements, to the food deficit areas. This holds good especially for countries like Thailand, Indochina, the Philippines and Hungary, where inflation has made the farmers unwilling to sell or produce at all.[1]

What we buy with such civilian goods is not only a saving for our food economy, but at the same time it means the creation of new markets for American goods used by low-grade consumer groups.

Our Federal Food Policy

After USDA and our farmers have performed the tremendous task of rescuing large parts of the world from starvation, the aims under the present situation will be to avoid any possibility of a recurrence of an emergency similar to the one experienced last spring. That means:

Maximize production of non-animal foodstuffs without consideration of the possibility that some surpluses may show up in the summer of 1947, and probably more in 1948 and later.

Keep the number and weight of meat animals under control so as to be able to export coarse grains for food and feed purposes and to accumulate a reasonable reserve of grains for possible smaller crops in the future.

Some measures which are still possible to increase *this year's feeds volume* are:

Pastures can be made to last longer, i.e., to yield more, if fertilizer is applied when a pasture is about used up. This was done widely in Europe. *It would not yet be too late to increase the yield.* Fertilizer can also be applied after the first cutting of hay.

Intermediary feed crops can be planted after the winter crops of wheat and oats have been harvested, where this is feasible, and where the fields are not used in other ways. Such crops are leguminose, sunflower and vetches. There is an ample supply of vetches seeds. Such crops yield protein-rich hay if the weather is favorable; otherwise they can be used for silage. If the weather should be unexpectedly bad, they can be plowed under as valuable fertilizer. Since the grain harvest is early, this possibility need not be considered.

This year's *very large potato crop* is in danger of being lost to a considerable extent for food and feeds, and for industrial purposes. Rapid progress with ensilage and with potato processing could add many million bushels of grain, which in any case would alleviate the food and feeds situation.

Production Goals to be Envisaged for 1946/47

1. Some of the goals have already been fixed. Some of them will not be published before September, when the real outcome of the crops will be clear. The wheat goal for 1947/48 is larger than in any war year.

2. It will be expedient to re-expand the acreage of soybeans, peanuts and other oil-bearing plants, and also to expand planting of sunflowers in the Unites States.

3. Secretary Anderson's wheat plan allocates 250 million bushels of wheat for export. There is little doubt that this can be filled without difficulty, and even exceeded. However, if a *modest reserve of coarse grains* could be accumulated in the hands of the CCC without any market disturbances during the first months of the year, it would demonstrate to the whole world that even if difficulties should arise in the late spring of 1947, no danger of a real food crisis exists.

4. Our fertilizer policy for 1946/47, first published in the European press, shows that USDA has attacked this vital question as energetically as possible. In the foreign press it was emphasized that we are going to produce 70,000 tons of nitrate per month, and that this in itself would mean an increase of 120 million bushels of wheat in the United States.

For all of 1946/47 we have allocated more than 300,000 tons of nitrate to Germany and Japan. The timing of these deliveries will be decisive for production possibilities in those countries, which still are the sore spots in the world (see appendix on chemical fertilizers.

Information which we personally obtained from the chemical industry indicated that the additional production during the first months might be considerably lower. This presents a difficult problem to our chemical industry; to choose between their domestic customers and the very great importance of their products to the food deficit nations.

Policy Concerning our Meat Animals

Hogs—The reduction set for the fall crop, namely 10% less than last year, will be more than achieved. This will provide less meat next spring, but help to increase or reserve coarse grains.

In spite of the much better feeds situation, everything should be done to avoid *a larger spring crop of hogs than the 52 million* which we had during the last two years.

Free markets may by themselves prohibit a too favorable ratio between grain and pork prices, which would lead to an overexpansion of our livestock and too heavy feedings. If not, everything should be done to prevent the over-feeding of hogs. If needed, this should be brought about by discounts for over-weight, an approach successfully applied for decades in Denmark, or by premiums or subsidies if the American approach is chosen.

Poultry—Exporting eggs instead of grains to hungry people is rather unwise, to say the least. Some 90% of the caloric value for the needy is then lost. Reduction of our overexpanded poultry flocks should be stimulated until we are sure that the next summer brings another good or at least medium harvest.

Cattle—No reduction of dairy cattle can be contemplated, but meat cattle should be reduced. However, if the high level of purchasing power should continue, the reduction cannot be very great.

The hope of Secretary Anderson, that the reappearance of consumer durable goods might divert a considerable amount of money from buying meat, may not be fully borne out by the facts.

However, it should be the aim that cattle should not be fed with the very best grades.

Your industry should therefore announce:
  a. That it does not need any wheat (as already begun by Mark Merritt, July 18, 1946).
  b. That in your processing, only part of the calories is lost and that the cattle feed value of the residual is increased.
  c. That you have new cattle feeding approaches to offer.
  d. That you back Herbert Hoover's plan to feed undernourished children.

The Hoover plan proposes an organization under the International Emergency Food Council to feed undernourished children everywhere:

All nations should be called to contribute to its cost. The job could be done with $300-400 million—a charge beyond the means of any organized private charity, but not a great sum for the world as a whole. (Ottawa, June 28, 1946)

Notes

1. For 1947/48, FAO emphasizes for the inflation-stricken rice-consuming nations: "Cotton textiles, thread, edible oils and fats, medicines, and fishing nets and hooks ... agricultural implements, barges, pumping units and spare parts for milling machinery."

Appendices

New Developments in Agriculture

The enormous war effort accelerated the pace of some important developments, which together have made possible the greatest production performance ever experienced in agriculture. These developments are very likely to increase our farm production still more in the coming years.

From 1939 to 1945 *we increased the volume of our agricultural production by about 35%, or almost 6% every year*, and we did this while 20% fewer persons were working on the farms.

The consequence was that per man-day we increased our output by more than 50%.

The graphs on the following pages give a picture of what has happened. This unheard-of achievement was brought about by:

1. Increased use of chemical fertilizer.

2. Increased use and improvement of farm machinery, and

3. Development of new seed varieties.

At present we need all of this increased productive power for ourselves, as well as to help the food deficit nations. The underlying forces, however, are so strong that *they will bring about fundamental changes in our total agricultural economy*.

One of them will be the recurrence of commodity surpluses.

Another will be a decrease in the farm population.

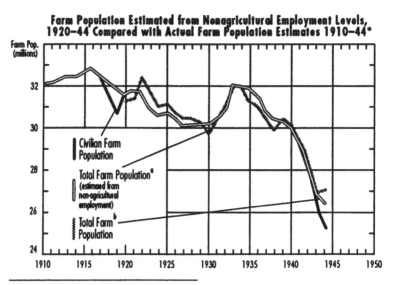

Farm Population Estimated from Nonagricultural Employment Levels, 1920–44 Compared with Actual Farm Population Estimates 1910–44*

Civilian Farm Population

Total Farm Population* (estimated from non-agricultural employment)

Total Farm[b] Population

*Farm population estimates for 1941–44 are tentative and subject to revision.
[b]Including persons who entered armed forces directly from a farm residence.

Source: U.S. Department of Agriculture

A third will be still greater productivity per acre and per farm worker, which should lead to a better diet for whole our population, and at lower prices.

Chemical Fertilizers

The Ultimate Nemesis of the World's Hunger

To the extent that agricultural techniques are able to overcome the effects of the greatest enemy of food production—drought—chemical fertilizers can increase the volume of human food to a level far beyond the world's present needs.

The increasing use of synthetic fertilizers has had a splendid effect on those countries in which they were first and most systematically used. In a recent reports some startling comparisons were shown:

1. Reduction in the manpower and acreage required to produce a given amount of food in Germany:

Year	Men	Acreage
1880	2.7	4.9
1937	1.0	2.1

2. Development of the average yield per acre in Denmark:

Year	Yield per Acre
Average 1919-23	25.8
Average 1924-28	31.9
Average 1929-33	35.5
1934	32.2
1938	37.1
1939	35.7

It was a generally accepted formula in Germany that the use of one extra ton of nitrogen would yield either 20 tons more of grain, 100 tons more of potatoes or beets, and 150 tons more of beet leaves.

The FAO has recently issued some new figures showing the soil's "response" to various types of fertilizers.[1] For example, in the United States it has been found that the use of *one ton of nitrogen* will produce an additional

20 tons of corn
15 tons of wheat
25 tons of barley or oats
30 tons of forage
37 tons of sweet potatoes
40 tons of potatoes
40 tons of vegetables

In India one ton of nitrogen produced 17 tons or rice, 36 tons of rice straw or 12.5–15 tons of wheat. Together with a light application of manure, one ton of nitrogen yielded 75 tons of potatoes, 25 tons of sugar and 275 tons of sugar cane.

Phosphoric acid and potash show results almost as spectacular. Thus, in Denmark one ton of phosphoric acid with dung produced 30.4 tons of sugar beet, and in Ireland 33.6 tons of potatoes.

In the United States one ton of phosphoric acid produced 23 tons of potatoes, 30 tons of forage and 30 tons of vegetables. On the other hand, one ton of potash produced 50 tons of potatoes, 45 tons of vegetables, 25 tons of forage and 15 tons of corn.

All of the above production figures are *in addition to* what the yield would have been without the use of the chemical fertilizers. While soils and the needs of soils vary, and sufficient moisture is always a prerequisite, the potentials of the use of chemical fertilizer appear at least to make future standards of nutrition dependent chiefly on the extent to which chemical fertilizers and irrigation are available.

World Production of Fertilizer

Considering these results, the present tendency to greatly increased use of fertilizer may well change the entire picture of the world's food economy.

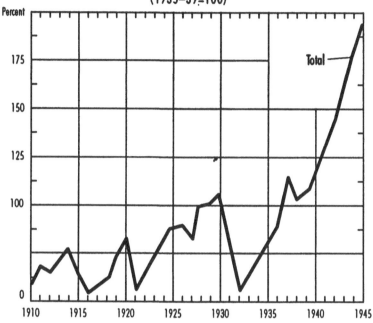

Fertilizer Consumption in Terms of Nitrogen, Phosphoric Acid, and Potash. Continental United States. 1910–45*
(1935–39=100)

*Computed from data supplied by P.I.S.A.E.A.A.A. and T.V.A.
Data for 1945 are estimated.

Source: U.S. Department of Agriculture.

The FAO goes so far as to say that on a world-wide basis the production of nitrate may reach a volume of 9 to 10 million tons per year in 10 years. If this were applied, we would have an additional crop of 150–200 million tons of wheat equivalent, or *120–150% more wheat than the world ever produced, even during its best periods.* As the world population is not expected to increase at a similar rate, the threat of mass starvation and malnutrition should disappear as soon as these possibilities are really utilized.

The actual application of fertilizers in the United States is shown in the following table:

Fertilizer Production in the U.S.

(Thousands of metric tons) Phosphates

	Nitrogen	Soluble	Rock	Potash
3-year prewar average	207	656	4101	276
1945-46	496	1435	5623	716
1946/47 estimate	515	1947	6100	726
FAO forecast for 1949/50	600		6000	800

As to nitrogen, this record for the United States is far below capacity. Most of the government-owned nitrogen factories have been closed down since the war. A large expansion is possible.

Industry experts from American Cyanamid demonstrated that the production capacity of private industry is 770,000 tons a year and of the government-owned plants 630,000 tons, which is a total production capacity of 1.4 million tons a year.

It is the considered opinion of experts in this industry that everything that can be produced in the United States can be sold this year. The problem will be to decide whether or not we would prefer to send larger quantities of chemical fertilizers abroad, or would rather send grain and other food products in quantities ranging from 20 to 100 times the tonnage of that chemical fertilizers would produce this food in Europe.

The fact that additional U.S. nitrogen plant capacity is going into operation, and is already showing marked results, is demonstrated by a press release from USDA dated July 12, 1946. It states that the supply of nitrogen allocated to American farmers for the 1947 crop will be 715,908 tons, compared with 699,118 tons for this year. That is already in excess of the nitrogen production capacity forecast by the FAO for 1949/50, and substantiates the potential plant capacity estimates of the American Cyanamid Company.

In addition to the above, 426,975 tons are allocated for export, including 330,000 tons for Germany and Japan.

Ratio of Hybrid Corn to Annual Corn Production
(in billion bushels)
1935–1946

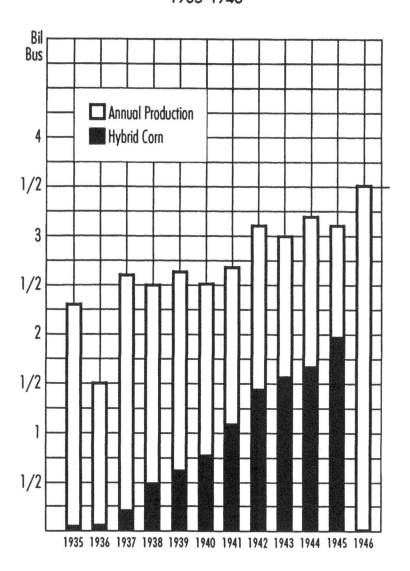

This would indicate a total supply of nitrogen fertilizer available in 1947 of 1,142,883 tons. Whether all of this is to be produced in the United States is not clearly indicated, but since some of the U.S. production is used for industrial purposes, it would appear that not much of our 1.4-million-ton capacity for nitrogen fertilizer is to remain unused.

At the same time, the supply of potash allocated to the U.S. farmers has been increased from 670,258 tons this year to 766,000 tons for 1947. The phosphate allocation has been increased from 7,318,613 tons to 8,333,333 tons for 1947.

It really looks as if the American farmer is going to make use of chemical fertilizers in a big way, and the effect this will have on the 1947/48 world food supply should not be minimized.

We will get more and more farm products from a less and less acreage than before. Nitrogen is extracted from the air; there is thus almost no limit to what we can produce.

A Note on Seeds

Plant Breeding

The *improved varieties of seed* had a very large share in the sensational increase of crops during the war. Although developed before the war, they have been utilized over wider and wider areas in the last years. Most important of all new seeds is the *hybrid seed corn*, which in 1945 replaced open-pollinated varieties on about 65% of the acreage planted. Hybrids, because of their greater vigor and their resistance to lodging, plant diseases and insects are credited with increasing the yield per acre by about 20% in 1944. It has been calculated that in 1944, when hybrid seeds were applied on 58% of the total corn acreage, corn production was 400 million bushels greater than it would have been if open-pollinated seed had been used on all of the acreage.[2] This seed was recently described as *the greatest innovation in the field of agriculture since the mechanical reaper.*[3]

Improvements have been made in oat seeds comparable to hybrid corn, but the improved varieties have not been so widely used. In recent years new varieties have contributed to the relatively high yields and have reduced abandonment. Much is expected from the introduction of the new strains over wider areas.

Crop Yields of Harvested Corn
and Oats Per Acre Harvested

		Corn	Oats
1880-99	*	25.9	27.9
1900-19	*	26.6	29.9
1920-29	*	26.8	29.7
1930-36	*	21.4	26.1
1937-41	*	28.9	31.6
1942		35.2	35.6
1943		32.1	29.6
1944		33.2	29.9
1945	**	32.0	32.0
1946	***		34.2
1950	***	38.8	38.5

* Average
** Probable
*** Potential, USDA estimate

The following figures show the increase of yields per acre since 1880. These increases, of course, are also due to agricultural techniques other than improved seeds.

We have seen similar successes with new varieties of wheat in Europe. For instance, Sweden formerly imported all of her wheat, producing only rye and oats. Then new strains of wheat were developed which could withstand the harsh northern climate, and these enabled Sweden to be self-sufficient in wheat during the war.

In this country the great expansion of soybean production is to a great extent due to the success of plant breeding.

The American seed industry stated with pride that it increased its output of vegetable seeds from 12 million pounds in 1939 to almost 353 million pounds in 1943, or an increase of 285% in four years.

Seed Hunger Overseas

Sending seeds overseas amounts to sending means of production. UNRRA reports to the FAO that the initial requests for seeds by the liberated areas was so great that the entire world supply would have been inadequate to meet them.

The demand for feeds import has been aggravated by the fact that toward the end of the war and later in distressed areas, hunger was so great that sufficient grain was not left for seed. UNRRA had to supply 383,000 metric tons of cereal seeds, 32,000 tons of forage crops and grasses, 17,000 tons of vegetable and dried legume seeds, and 68,000 tons of seed potatoes.

Our exports of fields seeds have much more than doubled in 1945/46, and approximately the same is the case for vegetable seeds. The USDA experts estimate that in 1946/47 we will still export more than before the war, but 25% less than last year.

Here is one of the most promising fields, and one in which scientific collaboration can bring help to the less developed nations.

The Role of Farm Machinery

Since the combined reaper and binder was invented in this country, the development of farm machinery has progressed steadily, but it never moved ahead as rapidly in volume and in variety as in the last few years.

Production of Farm Equipment
1929 to 1944
(in millions of dollars)

Year	Total Sales	Tractors only
1929	607	155
1931	214	98
1939	473	158
1941	746	349
1943	613	373

Production of farm machinery will undoubtedly reach a record level and is likely to increase even more during next year because

Farm Equipment Sold for Use in U.S.
(in million dollars)

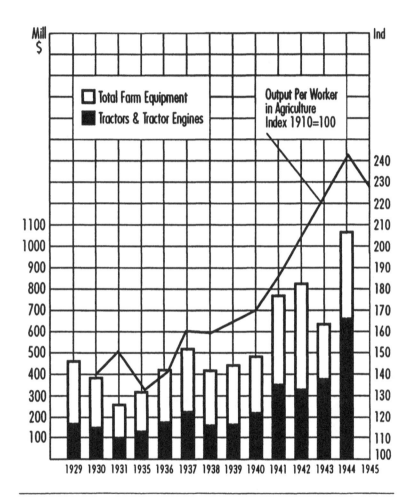

of the high purchasing power of the farmers, constantly rising farm wages, and the higher yield of farm machinery per dollar invested.

In his book "Sixty Million Jobs", Secretary Wallace predicted that the mechanical cotton picker alone would relieve 2 million laborers in the South. On dairy farms more farm workers will lose their jobs as soon as the milking machine takes over a still greater part of the work.' The number of milking machines has already doubled in four years, and has reduced the need for labor by half. Tractor mowers did 41% of the hay cutting in 1942, and will do as much as 50% this year. Larger hay crops have resulted from this help. Last year combines harvested 75% of our wheat and 4-% of our oat crops, as well as a good deal of the soybean crop. Mechanical corn pickers may harvest 60% of the corn crop this year.

The use of this machinery means less acreage needed to grow feed grains for horses and mules, better farming, and larger yields.

Shall We Send Our Tractors Abroad?

The problem is being discussed at present whether some of the agricultural machinery which will become available this year should be sent abroad. Tractors are in the front line of controversy. In the crop year 1945/46 farmers received 160,000 of them and figured that these had to replace 600,000 horses, which were the decrease of one year, and of which 75,000 had been sold to UNRRA. Since a tractor replaces about 4.5 animals for drawbar work, this means that almost 140,000 tractors served as replacements and only 20,000 of them could be counted as additional power.

For 1946/47, 240,000 tractors will be available and USDA wants to send 14,500 of them to Europe. The industry, especially the International Harvester Corporation, sharply objected to this plan as recently as July 23, emphasizing that the machines would go "largely to Russian-dominated countries".

The industry urges that the machines can be made in Europe, and that several of the nations which will receive them will not be able to operate or repair them. The European potential recipients argue that their soldiers learned how to handle such machinery. They hope to get tractors through UNRRA this fall, or at least used machinery.

If European agriculture is to be rehabilitated quickly, we should send all the farm machinery we can spare. However, it should be accompanied by good expert advice, for European soil conditions are much less uniform than those of the United States or Canada.

Notes

1. *Report on the World Food Situation*, Technical Supplement #7, mimeographed. Washington, DC, May 20, 1946.
2. U.S. Department of Agriculture, Bureau of Agricultural Economics, *Feed Grains and Meat Animals*, p. 5.
3. U.S. Department of Agriculture, *The Agricultural Situation*, July 1946.
4. See *Machinery on Farms, The Agricultural Situation*, U.S. Department of Agriculture, July 1946

Epilogue

Events soon confirmed the predictions of my 1946 research report. While temporary regional food shortages appear from time to time, such as the present one in Somalia, world-wide food shortages have never materialized; elaborate governmental agricultural product allocations have never been needed; and instead overproduction is becoming a major agricultural problem in more and more countries.

At a grain conference two years after my study, I elaborated on its long-term forecasts. My comments were reported in detail by *The Commercial and Financial Chronicle*. I would like to conclude this volume with a reproduction of that newspaper's May 20, 1948 report in full:

Food Surpluses Ahead: Mrs. Hirsch

Agricultural economist states in lieu of concern over Malthusian Law, public will shortly be complaining about food surpluses.

The wide-spread public fear that world food shortages will be permanent and that the Malthusian Law is proving valid after all is not justified by the facts, Mrs. Edith J. Hirsch, well known food authority and agricultural economist, declared on May 14. On the contrary, she predicted, within two years we are likely to be complaining about food surpluses.

Mrs. Hirsch whose predictions of world food needs and production were proved correct in 1946-47 and who late last fall forecast the break in grain and livestock prices which took place in February, spoke at the New School for Social Research on "World Grain Production and Price Spirals."

Mrs. Edith J. Hirsch

"I feel that we can safely forget about the Malthusian Law," Mrs. Hirsch asserted, "it is one of the theories which is revived after each war when the birthrate is temporarily high and when food shortages in the wake of war are acute." Already, Mrs. Hirsch said, we can see improvement—the European crop was good and reconstruction of agriculture has made progress everywhere. Even this year the shortages of wheat, sugar, and possibly feed grains may be over but there will remain a temporary shortage of oil seeds and "we would be doing a fine job if we were to increase our exports of oilcakes to Europe."

Our War Performance Scuttled Malthus

The strongest argument against the validity of the Malthusian Law, Mrs. Hirsch contended, is the astonishing war performance of our own agriculture which increased production during the war by 33%. Such a rapid increase is not possible in most countries, she admitted, since it pre-supposes an educational level which their farmers do not possess and ample research facilities. But the same rate of increase could be reached over a longer period of years especially since the aid of this country's research facilities is at the disposal of all countries wishing to make use of it.

International Wheat Agreement Questioned

Mrs. Hirsch expressed skepticism of the International Wheat Agreement negotiated by the government for the purpose of giving the American farmer an adequate share of world wheat exports. With both Argentina, the second largest prewar wheat exporter, and Russia and her orbit excluded from the agreement, we do not know whether it will work, she said. If it should work the American farmer would have an outlet of 1.1 billion bushels of wheat a year. Unfortunately, however, Mrs. Hirsch pointed out, the agreement may actually restrict the world's food production, since exporting countries will mould production policy to their export quotas and may leave insufficient margins for crop failures. Shortages and high prices of wheat are thus much more likely than if the world's farmers were allowed to make decisions for themselves. "We may very well be inviting food shortages by a world-wide grain cartel policy," she added.

Mrs. Hirsch was also critical of the claims that the diets of people in the underdeveloped countries can be quickly improved. This is a task which cannot be accomplished from the outside, she stated, but only by the countries themselves who must increase their own food production through better seeds and better farm techniques.

Index